best
easy
day hikes

Rocky Mountain National Park

Help Us Keep This Guide Up to Date

Every effort has been made by the authors and editors to make this guide as accurate and useful as possible. However, many things can change after a guide is published—trails are rerouted, regulations change, techniques evolve, facilities come under new management, etc.

We would love to hear from you concerning your experiences with this guide and how you feel it could be improved and kept up to date. While we may not be able to respond to all comments and suggestions, we'll take them to heart and we'll also make certain to share them with the authors. Please send your comments and suggestions to the following address:

The Globe Pequot Press

Reader Response/Editorial Department

P.O. Box 480

Guilford, CT 06437

Or you may e-mail us at:

editorial@GlobePequot.com

Thanks for your input, and happy travels!

A **FALCON** GUIDE®

Best Easy Day Hikes Series

best
easy
day hikes
Rocky Mountain
National Park

Kent and Donna Dannen

FALCON®

GUILFORD, CONNECTICUT
HELENA, MONTANA

AN IMPRINT OF THE GLOBE PEQUOT PRESS

AFALCONGUIDE®

Maps by Topaz Maps Inc. © The Globe Pequot Press

Library of Congress Cataloging-in-Publication Data

Dannen, Kent, 1946–
    Best easy day hikes, Rocky Mountain National Park / Kent Dannen, Donna Dannen.—1st ed.
        p. cm.—(A Falcon guide) (Best easy day hikes series)
    ISBN 0-7627-2272-X
        1. Hiking—Colorado—Rocky Mountain National Park—Guidebooks. 2. Trails—Colorado—Rocky Mountain National Park—Guidebooks. 3. Rocky Mountain National Park (Colo.)—Guidebooks. I. Dannen, Donna, 1949– II. Title. III. Series. IV. Series: Best easy day hikes series

GV199.42.C62 R622 2002
917.88'690433—dc21

                                                              2002067850

Manufactured in the United States of America
First Edition/Fourth Printing

Contents

Trails from Trail Ridge Road

West Side Trails

Winter Trails

Moraine Park Trails

Trails from Bear Lake Road

Map Legend

Symbol	Description	Symbol	Description
══(36)══	US Highway	▲	Campground
──(66)──	State Highway	🛈	Picnic area
════	Unimproved road	🛉🛉	Restrooms
▪▪▪▪	Route	🅿	Parking area
‑ ‑ ‑ ‑	Other trails	◻	Overlook
── ── ──	National Park boundary	⟨	Waterfall
〜	Stream	⌣	Mountain pass
Lake	Lake	▲	Summit
── ‑ ──	Continental Divide	⸗	Gate
		🚶	Trailhead

Overview Map

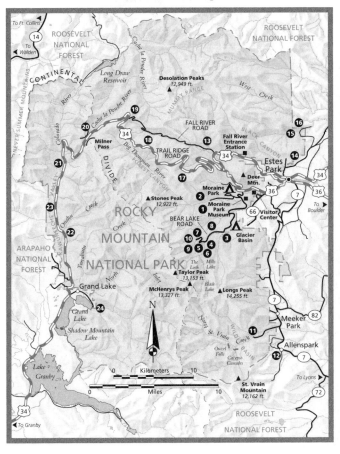

About the Cranky Authors

For a quarter century, guidebooks by Kent and Donna Dannen have been the standard reference for the trails of Rocky Mountain National Park. Therefore, many reviewers of their trail guides have accused the Dannens of being "experts."

This accusation offends the Dannens, who maintain that experts should never write guidebooks. For example, experts write user guides for VCRs, fax machines, and computers.

Experts lack ignorance and, therefore, lack the perspective of the ignorant, which is essential to explain anything. Because experts really do know all the answers, they have no clue about the questions. Guides written by experts are understood only by other experts, who rarely read them because they do not need to.

Although Kent and Donna Dannen admit to having hiked every trail in Rocky Mountain National Park, they also claim to have been lost often. Therefore, they know what the lost need to know and pass on that information in this guidebook. They fervently deny allegations that they are experts, except perhaps that they are expert at getting lost.

Introduction

Hikers can approach Rocky Mountain National Park hiking trails in several different ways. We have written our previous guidebooks for visitors who return often to the park's trails and who seek to know the trail systems broadly and intimately. Rocky Mountain National Park may be unique among America's parklands in the number of visitors who return again and again, year after year. These repeat visitors raise their families on park trails and, in part, remember family histories in terms of their experiences while hiking Rocky Mountain National Park.

We recently received a letter with two copies of a guidebook for us to autograph from a Chicago man. These were to be Christmas gifts for his grandsons (ages thirteen and sixteen), who had accomplished some rigorous hikes over the years. Evidently, these teens were asking for their own copies of our trail guide instead of relying on the various battered family editions. For him and thousands of other fans of Rocky Mountain National Park trails, we have written the ninth edition of *Hiking Rocky Mountain National Park.*

However, many other hikers on Rocky Mountain National Park trails seek only to sample the richness of this park before moving on to other jewels in the scenic treasure spread lavishly across North America. No one has the time or opportunity to devote all the attention deserved by such wonders as Yellowstone, Grand Teton, North Cascades, Grand Canyon, Yosemite, and on and on. Kent claims that whenever he visits Glacier National Park he gets mad—because he has to leave.

Consider not only the national parks but also national monuments, wilderness areas, state parks, and other public lands. Several lifetimes would be too short to appreciate them in depth. The decision merely to sample the glories of Rocky Mountain National Park trails is difficult to dispute. For samplers we have written *Best Easy Day Hikes Rocky Mountain National Park.*

The changing seasons also cause different approaches to Rocky Mountain National Park trails. The vast bulk of trail use is in the normally ideal weather of summer and fall. Winter, though, also charms some Rocky Mountain National Park enthusiasts. Although snowshoes and cross-country skis will never equal the popularity of hiking boots, the joys of winter in the backcountry are as impossible to exaggerate as are the joys of summer. For those lucky enough to find themselves ready for the short days, hypnotic light, and long nights of the park's longest season, *Best Easy Day Hikes* is also a guide to sampling park trails in winter.

Maps

For both summer and winter backcountry travel, you may desire larger maps than those in this book. The most informative topographic map for the entire park is the National Geographic Trails Illustrated recreation map of Rocky Mountain National Park. It comes in two forms, on recycled paper for $2.00 and on water-resistant paper for $10.00. It shows 80 feet between contour lines.

For a 40-foot contour scale, turn to United States Geological Survey quadrangle maps. These do not cover the entire park on one map. Each hike description includes the name of the quad (or quads) that cover that hike. Quads cost $4.00 each.

The Rocky Mountain Nature Association sells these maps either from outlets at park visitor centers or by mail. The toll-free telephone number for the mail order department is (800) 816–0108.

Bear Lake Shuttle Bus Service

Rocky Mountain National Park offers free shuttle bus service to transport visitors through the popular Bear Lake and Moraine Park areas. Visitors can avoid the congested Bear Lake parking lot by parking at the Glacier Basin parking area and catching the bus to Bear Lake. Hikers can use the bus as transportation between trailheads, facilitating one-way hikes, such as those beginning at Bear Lake and ending at Fern Lake Trailhead, Hollowell Park, Bierstadt Lake Trailhead, or Glacier Gorge Junction.

Bus service is daily in summer. The shuttle program goes to weekend-only service after Labor Day, serving visitors who want to view the aspens in their autumn colors during September. Schedules vary somewhat from year to year, but buses usually run every fifteen minutes from Glacier Basin in summer. The Moraine Park bus runs about once an hour.

The Bear Lake shuttle makes intermediate stops at Bierstadt Lake Trailhead and Glacier Gorge Junction. The Moraine Park loop starts at Fern Lake bus stop and runs to Glacier Basin parking lot with intermediate stops at Cub Lake Trailhead, Moraine Park Campground, Tuxedo Park, and Hollowell Park.

Since the shuttle began to run in 1978, proposals have been made to make its use compulsory for visiting Bear Lake during peak times. When or if compulsory use will be instituted is difficult to predict.

Leave No Trace Principles

From Backcountry/Wilderness Management Plan Rocky Mountain National Park, 2001

With increasing visitor use, both day and overnight, it is important to minimize our impacts and Leave No Trace of our visits into the backcountry. Please learn, practice, and pass on Leave No Trace skills and ethics to those you come in contact with. The following Leave No Trace principles will help protect precious backcountry resources.

Plan Ahead and Prepare

- Know and obey the regulations and special concerns for the area you'll visit.
- Be physically and mentally ready for your trip.
- Know the ability of every member of your group.
- Be informed of current weather conditions and other area information.
- Take responsibility for yourself and your group.
- Always leave an itinerary with someone at home.
- Choose proper equipment and clothing in subdued colors.

- Plan your meals and repackage food into reusable containers.

Travel and Camp on Durable Surfaces

While Traveling . . .
- Stay on designated trails and hike single file. Never shortcut switchbacks.
- When traveling cross-country, choose the most durable surfaces available: rock, gravel, dry grasses, or snow. Spread out so that you don't grind a path where one didn't exist before.
- When you stop to rest, be careful not to mash vegetation. Sit on rocks, logs, or in clearings.

At Camp . . .
- Be careful where you pitch your tent. Use the tent pad at the campsite, and camp in the camp area indicated on your permit.
- Restrict activities to the area where vegetation is compacted or absent.
- Use a large plastic water container to collect water so you don't need to make frequent trips to the water source.

Properly Dispose of Waste
- There are pit toilets at many backcountry sites. Use them.
- If there are no pit toilets nearby, urinate or defecate at least 200 feet (70 adult paces) from water, camp, or trails.

- Urinate in rocky places that won't be damaged by wildlife who dig for salts and minerals found in urine.
- Deposit human waste in catholes dug 6 to 8 inches deep. Carry a small garden trowel or lightweight scoop for digging. Cover and disguise the cathole when finished, or pack out solid waste.
- Use toilet paper sparingly and pack it out, along with sanitary napkins and tampons, in an airtight container.
- Wash your dishes and yourself at least 200 feet (70 adult paces) from water sources, and use small amounts, if any, of biodegradable soap. Scatter strained dishwater.
- Strain food scraps from wash water and pack them out.
- Pack everything you bring into the backcountry back out.
- Inspect your campsite for trash and evidence of your stay. Pack out all trash . . . *yours and others'.*

Leave What You Find

- Treat our natural heritage with respect. Leave plants, rocks, and historical artifacts as you find them.
- Good campsites are found, not made. Altering a site should not be necessary. Don't build structures or dig trenches.
- Let nature's sounds prevail. Speak softly and avoid making loud noises. Allow others to enjoy the peace and solitude of being in the backcountry.

Minimize Campfire Impacts

- Campfires are prohibited in the Rocky Mountain National Park wilderness except at certain designated

campsites where metal fire rings are provided.
- Campfires can cause lasting impacts to the backcountry. *Always* use a lightweight, portable stove for cooking. A campfire is a luxury, not a necessity.
- Enjoy the sounds and wonders of the darkness, or use a candle lantern instead of a fire.
- Where fires are permitted, use the metal fire grate. Don't scar large rocks by using them to enlarge the fire area.
- Gather *dead and down sticks,* no larger than an adult's wrist, from a wide area, and leave them in their natural form until you are ready to burn them. Scatter any unused sticks.
- Do not snap branches off live, dead, or downed trees.
- Put out campfires completely.
- Remove and pack out all unburned trash from the fire grate. Scatter the cold ashes over a large area well away from camp.

Respect Wildlife
- Enjoy wildlife at a distance.
- Never feed wildlife.
- Protect wildlife; hang your food and scented items securely.
- Minimize noise.
- Avoid sensitive habitat.

Be Considerate of Other Visitors
- Visit the backcountry in small parties. More people mean more impact.

- Avoid popular areas during times of high use.
- Avoid conflicts.
- Minimize noise.
- Keep a low profile.
- Take breaks and rest well off the trail, on a durable surface, of course.
- Yield to horse traffic.

For more information on Leave No Trace outdoor skills and ethics, contact the Backcountry Office or call LNT at (800) 332–4100. It's easy to enjoy and protect the backcountry simultaneously.

1
CUB LAKE

Type of hike: Loop.
Total distance: 6.3 miles.
Maps: Trails Illustrated; McHenrys Peak and Longs Peak USGS quads.
Highlights: Wildflowers, wildlife, Cub Lake (2.2 miles).
Wildlife: Many bird species (first half mile), mule deer, marmots, golden-mantled ground squirrels, many butterfly species.
Cub Lake elevation: 8,630 feet.
Trailhead elevation: 8,080 feet.

Finding the trailhead: From the Beaver Meadows entrance (US 36), drive 0.2 mile to the Bear Lake Road. Follow it 1.2 miles and turn right toward Moraine Park Campground. Follow the signs for 2.2 miles to the Cub Lake Trailhead and three reasonably convenient parking areas.

The hike: From the trailhead, hike south on the Cub Lake Trail, among the richest in the park for the wildflowers and wildlife seen along its length.

For much of its length across the level floor of Moraine Park, the trail is extremely easy to walk. Spoiled by the initial easiness of the trail, hikers may think the last half mile is rather steep.

Cub Lake

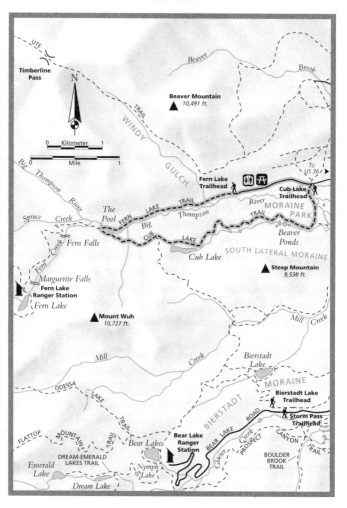

Jammed with innumerable opportunities for close-up photos, the Cub Lake Trail is not notable for its scenery, compared with much of the rest of the park. Low scenery potential and extremely abundant opportunities for studying small, intimate details that are abundant along the way to Cub Lake make this an ideal trail for cloudy-day hiking. Clouds may be welcome at the start of the trail, which offers scant shade. Insect repellent also may be beneficial.

The best view is looking toward Stones Peak from the east end of the lake, which is reached after 2.2 miles. Although a 1972 forest fire on the west end of the lake did nothing to help the vista, the plants growing back are an interesting study in plant succession after a fire or other disturbance. Note the masses of water lilies on the lake's surface denoting the gradual filling in of Cub Lake. Baby mallards among the lily pads are delightful; the lake's leeches (which don't prey on humans) are less lovely.

The Cub Lake Trail likely is the best place in Colorado to see rare, large, brilliant orange wood lilies, which bloom mainly during the first half of July. Hikers earlier or later in the summer are unlikely to be disappointed by the grand display of more common flower species.

Another 1.4 miles beyond Cub Lake, the trail meets the Fern Lake Trail, forming a circle route of 6.3 miles, including a mile of road walking between the Cub and Fern Lake Trailheads.

2
FERN FALLS

Type of hike: Out-and-back.
Total distance: 5.4 miles.
Maps: Trails Illustrated; McHenrys Peak USGS quad.
Highlights: Arch Rocks (1.5 miles), The Pool (1.7 miles), Fern Falls (2.7 miles).
Wildlife: Mule deer, chipmunk, red squirrel, water ouzel.
Fern Lake Trailhead elevation: 8,155 feet.
Fern Falls elevation: 8,800 feet.

Finding the trailhead: From the Beaver Meadows entrance of Rocky Mountain National Park on US 36, drive 1.2 miles on Bear Lake Road and turn right toward Moraine Park Campground. Drive another 0.5 mile and turn left just before reaching the campground. The pavement ends after 1.2 mile; continue 2 miles to the end of the unpaved road.

The hike: Like Fern Lake and Fern Creek, Fern Falls probably was named after a local lady rather than after the many bracken ferns that grow along the lower part of the trail, which follows a very easy grade along the Big Thompson River. These ferns are relegated to stream valleys, where moisture is readily available. Look closely at the lacy patterns of the fern leaves, which are particularly lovely in fall, when they turn a rusty golden color.

Fern Falls

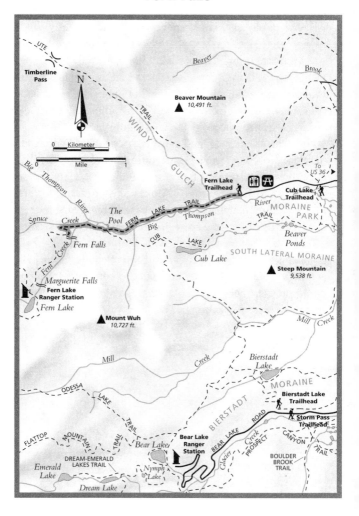

The Fern Lake Trail often emerges from the forest into meadows opened by beavers removing aspen. Throughout the warm months, these meadows produce many wildflowers that brighten the open spots with masses of color.

Arch Rocks, which probably fell from the cliffs above rather than being deposited by retreating glaciers, are interesting megaliths along the trail. The Pool is a wide spot where a bridge crosses the Big Thompson River, providing a sturdy platform for viewing swirling patterns of white water. Rock ledges at water's edge here often are nest sites for water ouzels, entertaining gray birds that live entirely within spray distance of water. An ouzel enters its moss-domed nest through a hole in the nest's side. You may find an inconspicuous nest by watching a bird repeatedly fly back and forth to the same spot along the stream.

The trail steepens a bit beyond The Pool, causing hikers to generate body heat even in forest shade. Fern Falls acts as an air-conditioner during the summer, throwing cool spray as Fern Creek bashes against the many tree trunks that lie across the falls.

3

SPRAGUE LAKE

Type of hike: Loop.
Total distance: 0.7 mile.
Maps: Trails Illustrated; Longs Peak USGS quad.
Highlights: Views of Front Range, beaver ponds.
Wildlife: Red squirrel, mallard duck, golden-mantled ground squirrel, gray jay, Steller's jay.
Sprague Lake elevation: 8,710 feet.

Finding the trailhead: The Sprague Lake Picnic Area is about 6.5 miles along Bear Lake Road from US 36. A sign indicates a turn to the left from Bear Lake Road.

The hike: The 0.7-mile trail around Sprague Lake is nearly flat and very easy to walk. It provides many opportunities for photography, especially early in the morning.

Gray jays, Steller's jays, and sometimes Clark's nutcrackers hang around the picnic area at the parking lot, waiting to steal unguarded morsels. Try to photograph these birds in the low branches that serve as their lookout points, giving a much nicer background than a picnic bench or the scantily vegetated ground.

Mallard ducks here are very tame and easy to photograph. Try for some action instead of the typical static pose: stretching a wing, interacting with other ducks, swimming among attractive shoreline grasses. Often you

Sprague Lake

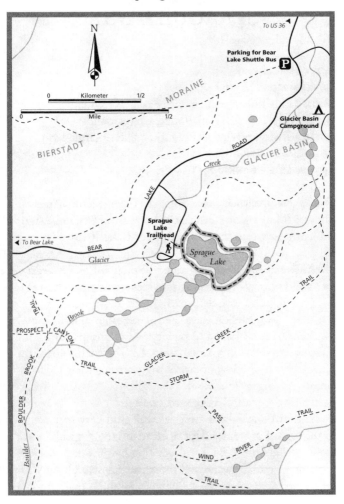

can photograph cute baby mallards at Sprague Lake. Try using them also as silhouettes in the foreground of pictures of the Front Range from the east side of the lake.

Walking around the lake provides at least two good perspectives of Otis Peak, Hallett Peak, and Flattop Mountain in the Front Range. The chances for reflections of the mountains on a still lake surface are excellent early in the day. The first good spot, if you begin walking left on the north side, is in a sheltered cove where a stream exits the thirteen-acre lake. Pines form a dark-shadowed frame for the mountains, the silhouetted needles filling empty sky with interesting shapes and directing the eye to the mountains.

Also here is one of the most photogenic blue spruces in the area. This single example of Colorado's state tree presents a classic cone shape when viewed from the east, across the water, and stands out nicely from the surrounding lodgepole pines.

The second good viewpoint of the Front Range is at the east end of the lake at its second outlet. There are few trees here to serve as good foreground for pictures of the mountains, but you can use bushes or flowers along the shore for this purpose. There also are some rounded boulders in the water near the shore, which were deposited by a melting glacier. The round shapes of these granite rocks make an interesting foreground element to add depth to your photo.

4
ALBERTA FALLS

Type of hike: Out-and-back.
Total distance: 1.2 miles.
Maps: Trails Illustrated; McHenrys Peak USGS quad.
Highlights: Alberta Falls (0.6 mile).
Wildlife: Mule deer, red squirrel, golden-mantled ground squirrel, chipmunk.
Glacier Gorge Junction elevation: 9,230 feet.
Alberta Falls elevation: 9,400 feet.

Finding the trailhead: Glacier Gorge Junction is 8.3 miles up the Bear Lake Road from US 36. If the parking lot is full, drive another 0.7 mile to Bear Lake's larger parking area and hike to Glacier Gorge Junction via a half-mile path (the horse trail) marked at the east end of the Bear Lake parking area or via a marked branch from the Dream Lake Trail just south of Bear Lake. Along the trail connecting Bear Lake and Glacier Gorge parking areas, late June hikers may encounter very rare brownie lady's-slipper orchids.

The hike: This easy path to a waterfall is one of the most popular short hikes in Rocky Mountain National Park. Along the way to Alberta Falls are many aspen that grew after a 1900 forest fire. Particularly with their fall color, these trees make this an extremely pleasant trail.

Alberta Falls

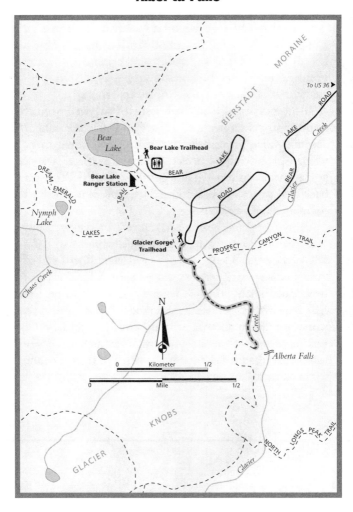

Heavy use has dictated that a certain percentage of the throngs, those who are ignorant of proper wilderness behavior, have carved their initials on the white aspen bark along this trail. Thankfully, most of this damage appears to be fairly old. The hiking public today seems to be more sophisticated about wilderness ethics, but even a tiny percentage of vandals can mess things up quite a bit.

Autumn aspens look their best when viewed from the southeast or southwest so your eyes catch the sunlight coming through translucent aspen leaves, creating a stained-glass-window effect. When leaves are backlit, golden color shimmers with greater intensity. With your back to the sun, you will notice duller autumn colors in all deciduous trees and bushes.

Abner Sprague, a pioneer and one of the first lodge owners in this area, named Alberta Falls for his wife. The falls plunge over a ledge gouged by glaciers. Other signs of glacial passing are boulders, gravel, light-colored clay, and bare bedrock smoothed by the moving ice. Also near the falls are now-dry potholes in the rock shaped by grinding stones carried by meltwater from retreating glaciers. This roaring torrent of ancestral Glacier Creek was much more formidable than today's stream, which still throws cooling spray on nearby hikers.

5
THE LOCH

Type of hike: Out-and-back.
Total distance: 5.4 miles.
Maps: Trails Illustrated; McHenrys Peak USGS quad.
Highlights: Alberta Falls (0.6 mile), The Loch (2.7 miles).
Wildlife: Mule deer, golden-mantled ground squirrel, pika, yellow-bellied marmot, gray jay, Clark's nutcracker, water ouzel.
Glacier Gorge Junction elevation: 9,230 feet.
The Loch elevation: 10,180 feet.

Finding the trailhead: Glacier Gorge Junction is 8.3 miles up the Bear Lake Road from US 36. If the parking lot is full, drive another 0.7 mile to Bear Lake's larger parking area and hike to Glacier Gorge Junction via a half-mile path (the horse trail) marked at the east end of the Bear Lake parking area or via a marked branch from the Dream Lake Trail just south of Bear Lake.

The hike: Estes Park pioneer Abner Sprague used a pun to name The Loch and Loch Vale, the valley in which this photogenic lake sits. He named these features for a guest at his lodge, a banker named Locke. Sprague changed the spelling to Loch, the Scottish word for lake, a clever joke that causes some confusion a century later. But many people who judge this to be the prettiest lake in

The Loch

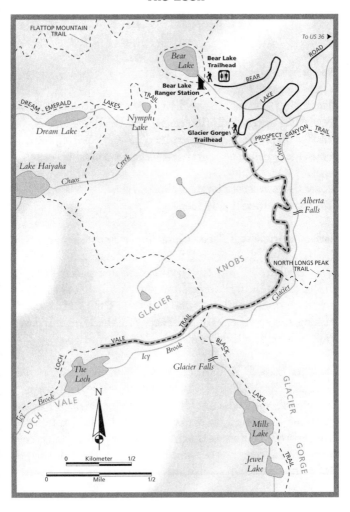

Rocky Mountain National Park think calling it The Lake is appropriate.

Named for Sprague's wife, Alberta Falls may be the most-photographed falls in the park. Beyond the falls the trail climbs amid rocks through land slowly recovering from a 1900 forest fire. Watch for colorful wildflowers growing against burned, weathered wood.

In the rock fields where the trail levels then descends slightly, marmots and pikas may whistle and chirp at passing hikers but likely will not permit close approach.

In a forested bowl missed by the 1900 fire, the trail splits three ways. A sign indicates the middle way to The Loch. A half mile beyond the junction, Icy Brook tumbles with a view of Taylor Peak above.

Taylor Glacier, nearby snowfields, and the Cathedral Wall dominate views from The Loch. Twisted limber pines on the rocky shore create a dramatic foreground.

6
MILLS LAKE

Type of hike: Out-and-back.
Total distance: 5 miles.
Maps: Trails Illustrated; McHenrys Peak USGS quad.
Highlights: Alberta Falls (0.6 mile), Mills Lake (2.5 miles).
Wildlife: Mule deer, golden-mantled ground squirrel, gray jay, Clark's nutcracker, pika, yellow-bellied marmot, water ouzel.
Glacier Gorge Junction elevation: 9,230 feet.
Mills Lake elevation: 9,940 feet.

Finding the trailhead: Glacier Gorge Junction is 8.3 miles up the Bear Lake Road from US 36. If the parking lot is full, drive another 0.7 mile to Bear Lake's larger parking area and hike to Glacier Gorge Junction via a half-mile path (the horse trail) marked at the east end of the Bear Lake parking area or via a marked branch from the Dream Lake Trail just south of Bear Lake. Take care crossing the road from the parking lot to the trailhead. This is the most hazardous part of the hike.

The hike: Mills Lake is named for Enos Mills, Father of Rocky Mountain National Park. Mills wrote many articles and books (some still in print) and gave many lectures urging the establishment of a national park around Longs

Mills Lake

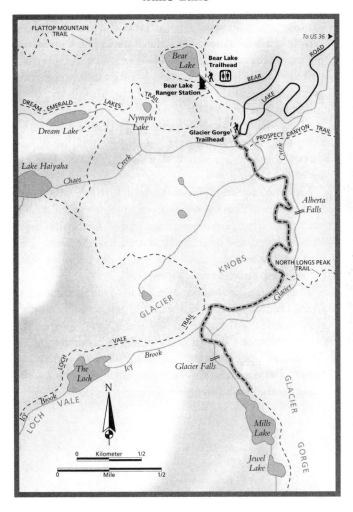

Peak. Six years of concentrated effort resulted in the park's creation in 1915.

Many hikers consider Mills Lake the prettiest lake in the park, a bold claim where there are so many outstanding contenders for this praise. Without doubt, this popular destination is extremely lovely in its dramatic setting below Longs Peak.

Along the first mile of the trail, Glacier Creek is exciting, especially where it shoots over Alberta Falls. Also along the first part of the trail, notice the weather-etched patterns in the grain of red, gray, and black wood killed in a 1900 forest fire.

Scrambling over glacier-scoured bedrock in Glacier Gorge, you will see several spectacular views of Longs Peak, tallest in the park, and the jagged Keyboard of the Winds. The round boulders left isolated on the bedrock by melting glaciers and the twisted shapes of limber pines increase the interest of this scene.

Unlike most lakes on the east side of the national park, Mills Lake is prettiest in the late afternoon. This fact alone is enough to merit praise from hikers who are tired of rising before dawn to see the best light on the peaks. Afternoon skies frequently contain clouds, which can either add interesting shapes to an empty sky or throw the entire landscape into shadow, making it all dull.

7
BEAR LAKE NATURE TRAIL

Type of hike: Loop
Total distance: 0.5 mile.
Maps: Trails Illustrated; McHenrys Peak USGS quad.
Highlights: Views of Hallett Peak and Longs Peak, natural history points of interest.
Wildlife: Mountain chickadee, red squirrel, golden-mantled ground squirrel, chipmunk, Steller's jay, gray jay, Clark's nutcracker.
Bear Lake elevation: 9,475 feet.

Finding the trailhead: Bear Lake is 9 miles from the Beaver Meadows entrance to Rocky Mountain National Park at the end of Bear Lake Road.

The hike: The paved, mostly level trail around Bear Lake is very popular. Nonetheless, it offers many opportunities for unspoiled views as well as photographs of the landscape, close-ups of patterns on tree trunks and boulders, wildlife portraits, and dramatic settings for people pictures.

Thirty-two numbered posts around the lake indicate points of interest, with short but informative descriptions in a booklet available from a dispenser at the east end of the lake. This reference is handy for anyone walking around Bear Lake. The more you know about what you

27

Bear Lake Nature Trail

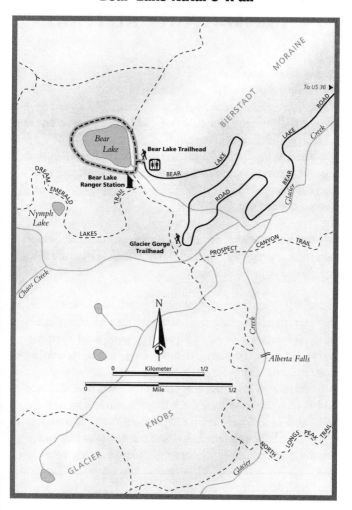

see, the more likely you are to enjoy it and to notice things you otherwise might have overlooked.

Early morning is the best time to view the east end of the lake, where most people congregate. Arriving early will help you avoid crowds and also enable you to view shadowed trees and boulders in the foreground as interesting silhouettes framing rugged cliffs above.

Heading counterclockwise around the lake will give you the most opportunities for interesting views of Hallett Peak. Fences protect some areas from trampling feet; walkers should stay on the paved trail. Also along the east side of the lake, look for interesting grain patterns in weathered limber pines. Be sure to notice the patterns of gneiss, a type of rock pointed out at stop ten.

Around stop twelve are magnificent views across the lake to Longs Peak and the other high mountains surrounding Glacier Gorge. This perspective of Longs is best enjoyed in late afternoon. Anytime of day, however, is a wonderful time to enjoy the beauty the Bear Lake area has to offer.

8
BIERSTADT LAKE

Type of hike: Shuttle.
Total distance: 3 miles.
Maps: Trails Illustrated; McHenrys Peak and Longs Peak USGS quads.
Highlights: Views of Hallett and Longs Peaks from Bear Lake, views of Longs Peak from Bierstadt Lake (1.6 miles), aspen along south side of Bierstadt Moraine.
Wildlife: Mule deer, elk, gray jay.
Bear Lake Trailhead elevation: 9,475 feet.
Bierstadt Lake Trailhead elevation: 8,850 feet.
High point between Bear and Bierstadt Lakes: 9,730 feet.

Finding the trailhead: Bierstadt Lake Trailhead is 6.4 miles along Bear Lake Road from US 36. Begin the hike at Bear Lake, 2.6 miles farther at the road's end.

The hike: Bierstadt Lake's formation may be unique among the lakes of Rocky Mountain National Park: It rests in a basin formed by the merging of two lateral moraines, rock ridges dumped by glaciers as they flowed down mountain valleys.

Most of the park's lakes were made by glaciers, but in ways that set them beneath scenic peaks. Bierstadt just sits in the midst of woods, although the view across from the north shore toward Longs Peak in the distance is not bad.

Bierstadt Lake

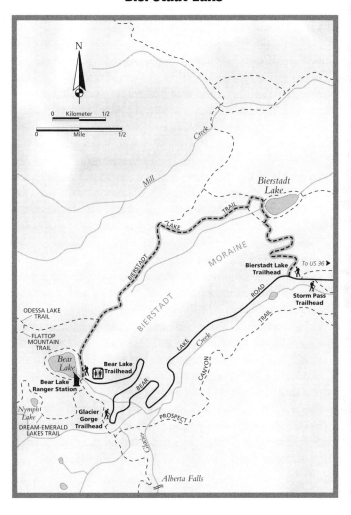

It seems ironic that comparatively mundane Bierstadt Lake was named after a nineteenth-century painter whose Rocky Mountain scenes were very grandiose.

The hike to the lake demonstrates how the journey can be more important than the destination. The best way is to begin at Bear Lake and follow a trail with only 255 feet elevation gain up Bierstadt Moraine. The nature trail around Bear Lake offers excellent views of Hallett Peak in the morning and an even better picture of Longs Peak in the afternoon. For the view of Longs, you need to walk past the Flattop Mountain Trail, which begins the trail to Bierstadt Lake, and continue for a few more yards around Bear Lake. Branching from the Flattop Mountain Trail 0.4 mile from Bear Lake, the Bierstadt Lake Trail continues climbing a short way through aspen to its high point. Then you descend through lovely woods to a gentle grade atop Bierstadt Moraine.

The area around Bierstadt Lake is a maze of trails, but signs provide adequate guidance. One trail circles the lake, another descends to Hollowell Park, a third heads down to the Bear Lake Shuttle parking area. But the best route of descent is to the Bierstadt Lake Trailhead on Bear Lake Road, 1.4 miles from the lake. Hikers reach the point of descent by following the trail around the lake's west end to a marked junction on the south side of the lake. From this junction, the Bierstadt Lake Trail switchbacks through open lodgepole pine and aspen woods that grew up after a 1900 forest fire. Nice at any time of year, this trail is magic in autumn when aspen leaves have turned golden.

Descending the trail causes hikers to face mostly south, increasing the richness of color in the aspen leaves as the sun shines through them. Mountains in the distance form interesting silhouettes, dark and brooding backgrounds that make the leaves stand out all the more brilliantly. The more dramatic peaks are to the southwest, making afternoon the most spectacular time on the south face of Bierstadt Moraine. Catch the shuttle back to Bear Lake or arrange for other transportation during the months when the shuttle does not run.

9
LAKE HAIYAHA

Type of hike: Out-and-back.
Total distance: 4.2 miles.
Maps: Trails Illustrated; McHenrys Peak USGS quad.
Highlights: Nymph Lake (0.5 mile), Dream Lake (1.1 miles), Longs Peak/Glacier Gorge views (1.6 miles), Lake Haiyaha (2.1 miles).
Wildlife: Mule deer, golden-mantled ground squirrel, chipmunks, yellow-bellied marmot, Clark's nutcracker.
Bear Lake Trailhead elevation: 9,475 feet.
Lake Haiyaha elevation: 10,220 feet.
High point of hike: 10,240 feet.

Finding the trailhead: From the Beaver Meadows entrance to the park, take US 36 to Bear Lake Road and drive 9 miles to the road's end at the Bear Lake Trailhead.

The hike: The first half of the hike to Lake Haiyaha follows one of the most popular (and crowded) trails in Rocky Mountain National Park. Avoid the crowds and experience the trail at its best by starting early in the day, as soon after sunrise as you can bear.

At the beginning of the hike, there are striking views of Hallett Peak above Bear Lake, seen by detouring a few yards from the Dream Lake Trail. The best views at Bear

Lake Haiyaha

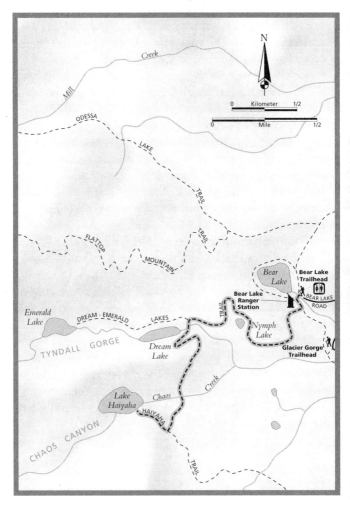

Lake probably are a short distance to the right from where you reach the shore.

The hike to Haiyaha begins on the Dream Lake Trail a short way south (left) from Bear Lake. You will see some nice views of Longs Peak and Glacier Gorge framed by aspen on the way to Nymph Lake, but even better views are at Nymph and beyond. Nymph Lake offers a perspective of Hallett and Flattop Mountain different from Bear Lake's. Water lilies float on Nymph's surface.

Abstract grain patterns on burned and uprooted limber pines along the north shore are worth noting. Interesting trees around the lake frame lovely views of Thatchtop Mountain and Longs Peak. Watch for other interesting views of Longs Peak from the trail between Nymph and Dream Lakes.

The best morning scenes of the hike are at Dream Lake. At a trail junction a bridge crosses Tyndall Creek; turn right before crossing the bridge. At Dream Lake, 0.1 mile from the bridge, wind-shaped limber pines frame views of Hallett and Flattop. A wide-angle lens typical on most point-and-shoot cameras works well here.

Return to the bridge across Tyndall Creek and continue up switchbacks through a grand subalpine forest. Breaking into the open, the Lake Haiyaha Trail bends around a ridge with good views of Bear and Nymph Lakes, followed by better views of Longs Peak and Glacier Gorge.

A quarter mile before Lake Haiyaha, a connecting trail to Glacier Gorge provides access to many hiking destinations and a longer route back to Bear Lake.

Descend to cross Chaos Creek and bear right through large boulders to Lake Haiyaha, whose Native American name is said to mean "big rocks." The view of Hallett here is less exciting than from the other lakes, but a giant limber pine here is one of the most spectacular examples of this species that we have ever seen.

10
EMERALD LAKE

Type of hike: Out-and-back.
Total distance: 3.6 miles.
Maps: Trails Illustrated; McHenrys Peak USGS quad.
Highlights: Views of Hallett Peak, Flattop Mountain, and Longs Peak with pond lilies at Nymph Lake (0.5 mile), limber pines framing Hallett and Flattop at Dream Lake (1.1 miles), Emerald Lake (1.8 miles).
Wildlife: Mule deer, chipmunk, golden-mantled ground squirrel, gray jay, Clark's nutcracker.
Bear Lake Trailhead elevation: 9,475 feet.
Dream Lake elevation: 9,900 feet.
Emerald Lake elevation: 10,080 feet.

Finding the trailhead: Bear Lake is at the end of 9-mile-long Bear Lake Road, which begins near the Beaver Meadows entrance of Rocky Mountain National Park (US 36).

The hike: Because this trail gives hikers a great deal of spectacular scenery with relatively little effort, it is the most crowded path in Rocky Mountain National Park. Avoid crowds and see the trail at its best by starting to hike before sunrise. Starting early will provide the most dramatic light on the peaks and probably little wind. You also will meet more animals along the trail. The uphill hiking temperature will be cool and trailhead parking is no problem!

Emerald Lake

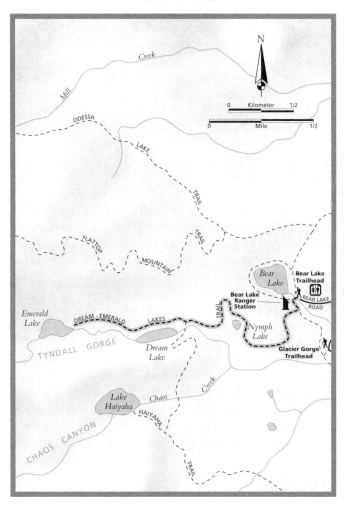

Even by flashlight beam, signs marking the trail to Nymph and Dream Lakes are easy to follow. If you start at the ideal time, it will be too dark for photos at Nymph Lake when you arrive, but you can catch it on the way back.

On your return try a wide-angle lens to use trees on the east shore to frame a photo of Hallett Peak, Flattop Mountain, and the lily pads on the lake surface. Perhaps the trees on the shore will still be in shadow and can be made a silhouette in front of the brightly lit peaks. Be sure to take your light reading off the brightest part of the picture, probably the sky.

Use the same principle to shoot Longs Peak from the trail on the north side of the lake. Just as the trail bends around Nymph's north edge, watch for upended tree roots and burned limber pine trunks, which make grand subjects for close-up abstract photos. Along the trail, the slopes above Nymph Lake are good spots for wildflower photography, somewhat sheltered from wind.

At the Lake Haiyaha Trail junction, keep to the right toward Dream Lake. The lake is the ideal place to be at sunrise, when alpenglow spreads rich colors of changing hues across the faces of Hallett Peak (on the left) and Flattop Mountain. A wide-angle lens will be very useful for including the dark, wind-twisted forms of limber pines or companion hikers in the foreground, below the sharp spires of Flattop. The mountain's name may seem perverse, but viewpoint is everything. From a distance, it really is flat and dull-looking. From this trail, the glacier-carved flank is the last word in drama.

Try to use divisions of light and dark within your view of Dream Lake to divide the picture vertically into thirds, and avoid making the surface of the lake a line that cuts the picture in half.

Continue 0.7 mile to Emerald Lake. Watch for views of Tyndall Creek tumbling over bedrock accented by clumps of wildflowers below Flattop.

11
OUZEL FALLS

Type of hike: Out-and-back.
Total distance: 5.4 miles.
Maps: Trails Illustrated; Allens Park USGS quad.
Highlights: Abundant wildflowers (first half mile), noisy white-water stream (first 1.3 miles), Calypso Cascades (1.8 miles), regrowth after 1978 forest fire (2 miles), Ouzel Falls (2.7 miles).
Wildlife: Mule deer, red squirrel, chipmunk, yellow-bellied marmot, golden-mantled ground squirrel, water ouzel.
Wild Basin Trailhead elevation: 8,500 feet.
Calypso Cascades elevation: 9,200 feet .
Ouzel Falls elevation: 9,450 feet.

Finding the trailhead: Follow Colorado Highway 7 more than 11 miles south of Estes Park to a well-marked road into Wild Basin (about 2 miles are unpaved and narrow).

The hike: Although dawn or earlier is usually the best time to start hiking in Rocky Mountain National Park, this painful practice is unnecessary for a hike to Ouzel Falls, which does not exhibit significant mountain views.

The low, bright light of early morning that illuminates mountain vistas so dramatically is not the best for viewing shady streamside vistas along the trail to Wild Basin's most popular hiking destination. Sunny skies pour too

Ouzel Falls

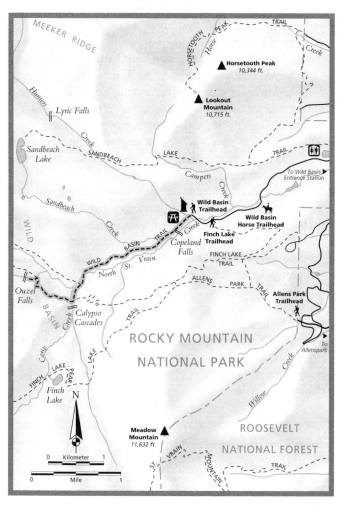

much light on raging white streams, making so much contrast between water and woods that it is very difficult for your eyes to perceive the whole scene at once. Toward midday the sun will be higher in the sky and often dimmed by clouds, casting even light by which it is easier to appreciate the wonders of Wild Basin forests.

The lower light level under cloudy skies also permits photographers to steady their cameras on tripods, rocks, or bridge railings to use a slow shutter speed $\frac{1}{15}$ or $\frac{1}{8}$ second). This slow speed allows moving water to flow into fuzziness while surrounding solid objects remain still during the opening of the camera shutter.

The Wild Basin trails are rich in wildflower species. Watch in particular (in early July) for small pink calypso orchids at trailside near Calypso Cascades. A shaft of sun may penetrate the shade to spotlight one of these orchids.

The burned area beyond Calypso Cascades exhibits the lush green of shrubs and flowers that grew up after forest shade was removed. You are likely to see deer here, as well as marmots and ground squirrels. Appropriately, fireweed is very abundant, but deer often eat its bright magenta blossoms, disappointing hikers who expect to enjoy masses of color. The colors of flowers, leaves, and burned wood blend more pleasingly under overcast rather than sunny skies.

At the bridge over Ouzel Creek below Ouzel Falls, leave the main trail to climb to the base of the falls. Here you may find the falls graced by the presence of colorful wildflowers.

Ouzel Falls is named for a dull gray bird, a bit smaller than a robin and shaped like a wren. Ouzels also are called dippers because they fly from under the water to land on a rock and perform an entertaining bobbing dance. They stay in the water or just above it rather than flying over the land. You are likely to see them along any of Wild Basin's streams.

12
ALLENS PARK TRAIL TO CALYPSO CASCADES

Type of hike: Out-and-back.
Total distance: 6.2 miles.
Maps: Trails Illustrated; Allens Park USGS quad.
Highlights: Forest fire of 1978, interesting trail building, views of Longs Peak, Calypso Cascades (3.1 miles).
Wildlife: Red squirrel, chipmunk, golden-mantled ground squirrel, mountain chickadee, Steller's jay, gray jay, mule deer.
Allens Park Trailhead elevation: 8,520 feet.
Calypso Cascades elevation: 9,200 feet.

Finding the trailhead: From Colorado Highway 7, turn south on Business Highway 7 (Washington Street) into the town of Allenspark. Drive one block and turn right onto unpaved County Road 90. After 0.7 mile, bear left uphill on South Skinner Road. After a half mile, turn right on Meadow Mountain Drive and continue a short distance to the Allens Park Trail parking area on the right.

The hike: Calypso Cascades is a popular destination in Rocky Mountain National Park, but by starting at the Allens Park Trailhead, the hike to the cascades is free from the bustle of crowds until you reach the destination. The trail offers interesting scenery opened by a 1978 forest fire.

Allens Park Trail to Calypso Cascades

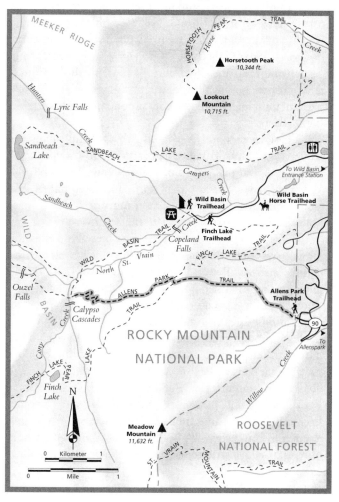

Whereas hiking the main trail in Wild Basin is a streamside experience, hiking Allens Park Trail is a study of the effect of forest fire. In 1978 a lightning-generated fire swept through Wild Basin. A good deal of the burning occurred on the side of Meadow Mountain along which the trail runs. The burn opened up the old forest and created spectacular views of Longs Peak, Pagoda Mountain, Chiefshead, and the mountains at the head of Wild Basin.

These views appear beyond the first junction along the Allens Park Trail. To take the best route to Calypso Cascades go left at this junction. The views are lovely, but the openness makes this a rather warm and steep hike unless you begin early in the day, when morning light is most lovely on the incredible views to the northwest.

Trailside vegetation has changed since the forest fire. Now, large areas of the trail are lined with pioneering shrubs and wildflowers that attract deer and elk. Small, new stands of aspen also have appeared, utilizing the sunny hillside habitats and paving the way for the next generation of plants to take root.

The fire did more than damage the forest vegetation, however. Burning into the soil itself and denuding the forest floor, it caused great erosion along the trail, especially near Confusion Junction where the Finch Lake and Allens Park Trails divide. Just beyond the junction, some extreme trail building measures hold the erosion at bay. Along one stretch of trail, where log walls seem to shore up a whole mountainside, a spectacular view of Longs Peak is visible.

Not far beyond, the trail enters undisturbed primeval forest typical of much of Wild Basin. The contrast is quite stunning, cool, and fragrant. An elaborate bridge with stone pavement on each side crosses an unnamed creek before you descend several switchbacks to the junction with the main Wild Basin Trail at Calypso Cascades.

13
FALL RIVER ROAD

Type of hike: Shuttle (out-and-back to Chasm Falls).
Total distance: 9 miles (5.2 miles out-and-back to Chasm Falls).
Maps: Trails Illustrated; Fall River Pass and Trail Ridge USGS quads.
Highlights: Chasm Falls (2.6 miles in winter), avalanche site (4.8 miles).
Wildlife: Mule deer, elk.
West Alluvial Fan parking lot elevation: 8,250 feet.
Chasm Falls elevation: 9,060 feet.
Fall River Pass elevation: 11,796 feet.

Finding the trailhead: In the spring, when Trail Ridge Road reopens (probably some time in late May), hikers can leave one car at Fall River Pass on Trail Ridge Road and another near the bottom of Old Fall River Road at the West Alluvial Fan parking area.

From the park's Fall River entrance, follow US 34 for 2.1 miles to the Fall River Road turnoff. The West Alluvial Fan parking area is 0.8 mile along Fall River Road (past the first parking area labeled "Alluvial Fan").

The hike: Old Fall River Road was the first motorized route to transect Rocky Mountain National Park, opening in 1920. Many centuries earlier, however, Arapaho travelers

Fall River Road

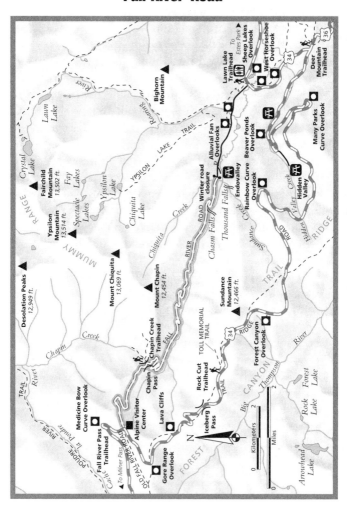

called this the Dog Trail because their dogs pulled travois bearing the Native Americans' burdens over this route to the other side of the mountains.

Today, from the first Saturday in April until road crews reopen Fall River Road after winter closure (probably early July), it is one of the few places in this national park where hikers can re-create this human-canine partnership with dog packs. To preserve this opportunity for everyone, hikers absolutely must keep their dogs leashed according to park regulations.

In winter, Chasm Falls, a 2.6-mile walk along closed paved and unpaved roads, is a good safe hike. The nearest winter trailhead is 1.2 miles from the old road at the West Alluvial Fan parking lot. Exactly when winter ends is hard to determine. Absence of road closure may enable you to park closer (in small roadside parking spots) in spring and early summer.

This is one of the park's best areas to see elk, as indicated by the heavy black scarring of aspen trunks along the paved road that runs along the Fall River valley floor. Elk strip off the bark for winter food.

The right turn up unpaved Old Fall River Road is obvious. From the start of the unpaved road it is another 1.4 miles to Chasm Falls, where potholes at the base of the falls were scoured thousands of years ago by glacial meltwater dropping through ice cracks and swirling rocks. Fall River continues the same process at the base of the 25-foot falls. Be very careful of steep, slick surfaces when you are near the falls.

Care also is needed when hiking beyond the falls after heavy snows, which can occur well into May. In 1985–86 a major avalanche snapped off many large trees, visible in a jumbled mass as you look right up the slope of Mount Chapin, 2.3 miles beyond the falls. This avalanche had not run for many decades. No one knows when or where the next unpleasant surprise may roar across the road, but particular care is necessary after heavy snows. Avalanche danger probably increases with altitude as far as Chapin Pass Trailhead, 8 miles from the Alluvial Fan.

Above Chasm Falls, watch for bighorn sheep on rock outcrops north of the road. Elk often appear on the road itself and across the valley on the side of Sundance Mountain.

After Trail Ridge Road reopens, probably in late May, hikers have access to Fall River Pass and can hike downhill all the way to Horseshoe Park. This is a great hike in June, passing through all of the national park's life zones, but requires arranging transportation at both ends of Old Fall River Road.

14
GEM LAKE

Type of hike: Out-and-back.
Total distance: 3.6 miles.
Maps: Trails Illustrated; Glen Haven and Estes Park USGS quads.
Highlights: Unique rock formations, views of Longs Peak above Estes Valley, Gem Lake (1.8 miles).
Wildlife: Mule deer, Richardson ground squirrel, golden-mantled ground squirrel, white-throated swift.
Twin Owls Trailhead elevation: 7,920 feet.
Gem Lake elevation: 8,830 feet.

Finding the trailhead: From downtown Estes Park, follow MacGregor Avenue north about a mile to the ranch gate. Enter and continue 0.8 mile on the pavement to the trailhead. *Note:* The National Park Service has proposed building a new Gem Lake Trailhead and eliminating the Twin Owls and smaller Gem Lake trailheads. If this is done, the new trailhead will be well marked along Devils Gulch Road and a new trail about 0.7 mile long will connect the new parking area with the current Gem Lake Trail near Twin Owls.

The hike: Popular throughout the year, Gem Lake is a particularly good hike for folks eager to experience spring on the trail. In Rocky Mountain National Park, the Gem Lake Trail sees spring first. Here is the place to observe

Gem Lake

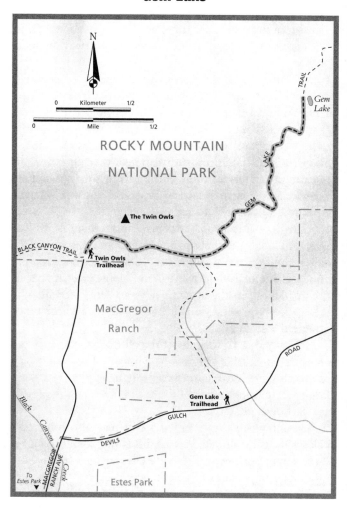

pasqueflowers pushing their purple tulip heads through the forest duff. Watch for bitterbrush blooming first near the surface of rocks that are solar collectors, radiating heat to create early spring before the season arrives for most other plants.

Even the most unimaginative of hikers can see a pair of owls in the two huge granite pillars that rise above the trailhead on Lumpy Ridge. Equally obvious is Paul Bunyan's Boot about halfway to Gem Lake. Wind and mildly acidic rain have sculpted countless other abstract monoliths along the trail into formations fascinating to both romantic and prosaic minds. It is a natural playground for children, but parents need to supervise and warn kids to avoid falls from slick rocks.

Gem Lake is a small jewel in a big setting. Actually a large (0.2 acre) pothole in the granite, it has no inlet or outlet and averages a foot deep. Its beauty, therefore, is more subtle than that of the grand alpine lakes higher in the park. Notice the abstract color patterns of lichens at the base of the cliffs on the north shore. Limber pines frame the distant peaks.

Weathering of rocks atop the cliff above the lake has created remarkable patterns of potholes. The easiest way to reach these is to clamber very carefully up the less steep slope around the corner of the rock bulwark on the north side of the lake.

Climbing to the top of the cliff may also bring you closer to white-throated swifts, birds that look like cigars with swept-back wings. They dart at very high speeds over the water in pursuit of flying insects.

15
BRIDAL VEIL FALLS

Type of hike: Out-and-back.
Total distance: 6 miles.
Maps: Trails Illustrated; Estes Park USGS quad.
Highlights: Aspen-lined Cow Creek, Bridal Veil Falls (3 miles).
Wildlife: Elk, mule deer.
Cow Creek Trailhead elevation: 7,840 feet.
Bridal Veil Falls elevation: 8,900 feet.

Finding the trailhead: From downtown Estes Park, follow Devils Gulch Road 3.9 miles to McGraw Ranch Road. Turn left and drive 2.3 miles to the Cow Creek Trailhead at the end of this unpaved road. Parking is only permitted in the parking area at the trailhead. Do not park along the road beyond the ranch boundary.

The hike: Cow Creek presumably was named for the livestock at McGraw Ranch, established in 1874. The cattle were gone long before McGraw Ranch became part of Rocky Mountain National Park in 1988. There were many cows along Cow Creek nonetheless—cow elk and admiring bulls, of course.

You have an excellent chance of spotting elk along Cow Creek on the way to Bridal Veil Falls, particularly in winter, so if you have a telephoto lens and tripod, haul

Bridal Veil Falls

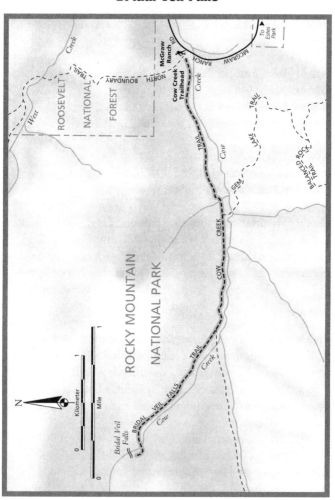

them along. The extra effort could yield a prizewinning photo.

Fortunately, the trail to the falls seems relatively easy. The path meanders west from the trailhead, usually staying in the open meadows that are vital sources of food for elk. Usually free of winter snow, the path can be rather warm in the summer. Using sunscreen is a good idea throughout the year.

Hikers need not be particularly observant to see that the elk do not feed only on the grass. They also eat willows and streamside shrubs. The black scars on aspen bark are particularly obvious signs of elk dining. The double vertical scars show where elk use their lower incisors to strip bark from the trees. Light-colored wood indicates more recent feeding; it eventually turns black. The rough black scars contrasting with the smooth, nearly white aspen bark can create some interesting patterns for close-up photography.

Beavers also feed on the aspen and use it extensively to construct dams and lodges. Many beaver ponds slow the flow of Cow Creek, providing excellent opportunities in fall for reflection photos of aspen gold.

Actually spotting the beavers themselves will be a matter of luck. They are in significant danger from predators when they are out of the water, and they tend to do most of their cutting at night. They are most active in summer and fall, when they store aspen and willow branches and trunks under the surface of the water. After winter freezes the surface, they reach their stores by an underwater entrance from their den or lodge.

Bridal Veil Falls is one of the prettiest in the park. It is especially spectacular in spring, when the torrent of melting snow rushes over the falls with so much force that the water gushes back into the air from the pool below the falls. In winter, the more subtle beauties of frozen splashes and streamside ice patterns create a lovely setting.

16
WEST CREEK FALLS

Type of hike: Out-and-back.
Total distance: 4 miles.
Maps: Trails Illustrated; Glen Haven and Estes Park USGS quads.
Highlights: McGraw Ranch, West Creek Falls (2 miles).
Wildlife: Mule deer, elk, red squirrel.
Cow Creek Trailhead elevation: 7,840 feet.
West Creek Falls elevation: 8,160 feet.
High point: 8,440 feet.

Finding the trailhead: From downtown Estes Park, follow Devils Gulch Road 3.9 miles to McGraw Ranch Road. Turn left and drive 2.3 miles to the Cow Creek Trailhead at the end of this unpaved road. Parking is only permitted in the parking area at the trailhead. Do not park along the road beyond the ranch boundary.

The hike: McGraw Ranch, one of the oldest in this area, was established in 1874. Cow Creek gained its name soon after, presumably from the stock on the ranch. Various architectural details of the ranch structures make good photo subjects and backgrounds for portraits.

Even a century ago, it was obvious that catering to tourists made more economic sense than catering to cows.

West Creek Falls

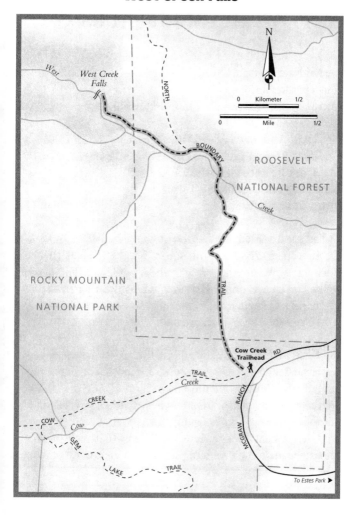

McGraw Ranch enabled many guests to experience the beauty of its out-of-the-way valley.

The back of a horse was the favored vantage point of these guests. Just west of the ranch buildings, the North Boundary Trail to West Creek Falls heads right up a ridge, the route of guests content to let horses do the puffing and panting.

From the low point on the ridge between West and Cow Creeks, the trail weaves back and forth steeply down through a Douglas-fir forest to West Creek. Across the creek, head left (west) at a trail intersection and walk a gentle grade along the bank to West Creek Falls. In this peaceful setting of a rocky amphitheater, the creek descends in two tiers.

17
TIMBERLINE PASS

Type of hike: Out-and-back.
Total distance: 4 miles.
Maps: Trails Illustrated; Trail Ridge and McHenrys Peak, USGS quads.
Highlights: Open vistas, various tundra environments with many flower species.
Wildlife: Water pipet, horned lark, pika, yellow-bellied marmot, elk.
Ute Crossing elevation: 11,440 feet.
Timberline Pass elevation: 11,484 feet.

Finding the trailhead: Ute Crossing is just above tree line, 2 miles above Rainbow Curve and 0.8 mile downhill from Forest Canyon Overlook. There is additional parking a short walk up Trail Ridge Road from Ute Crossing.

The hike: This is a section of the Old Ute Trail (called the Child's Trail by the Utes), which extends across the Continental Divide from Estes Park to Grand Lake. Trail Ridge Road overlays much of this ancient past.

From the Ute Crossing on Trail Ridge Road, a delightful and easy tundra walk passes through most of the tundra plant communities: disturbed areas, snow-accumulated areas, mature meadows, marshes, and krummholtz (wind-distorted trees). A good destination is

Timberline Pass

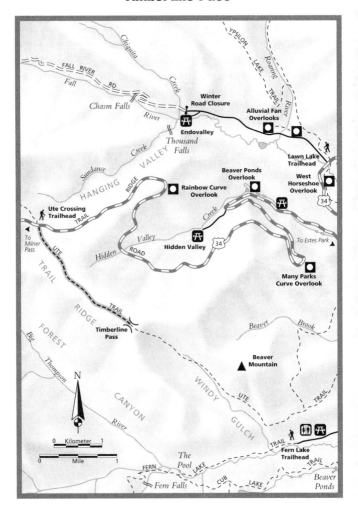

a tor—a mass of disintegrating, flower-filled bedrock—in Timberline Pass.

As the trail undulates across the tundra south of the road, hikers' eyes naturally turn to the highly glaciated peaks to the south (right) rising near at hand above track-less Forest Canyon and farther away above the Bear Lake area and Glacier Gorge. The flat-topped tower that rises above all others far to the south is Longs Peak, the highest mountain in the national park at 14,255 feet.

Scattered along the trail are more tors that caused this part of Trail Ridge to be called Tombstone Ridge. This ominous name might remind you to retreat to your cars if storm clouds build. There is no protection from lightning along the ridge.

Hike early in the day to avoid storms and reduce wind disruption of flower photography. Because tundra plants have no protection from trampling feet, stay on the path between piled-up rock markers (cairns) as much as possible. When investigating a point of interest away from the path, step on rocks and avoid other hikers' footsteps.

18
TOLL MEMORIAL

Type of hike: Out-and-back.
Total distance: 0.8 mile.
Maps: Trails Illustrated; Trail Ridge USGS quad.
Highlights: Alpine plants, Mushroom Rocks (0.25 mile), Toll Memorial peak finder (0.4 mile).
Wildlife: Yellow-bellied marmot, pika, chipmunk, raven, Clark's nutcracker.
Rock Cut Trailhead elevation: 12,110 feet.
Toll Memorial elevation: 12,310 feet.

Finding the trailhead: Rock Cut Trailhead is well marked along Trail Ridge Road 12.5 miles from the junction of US 34 and US 36.

The hike: Rock Cut is the highest trailhead in Rocky Mountain National Park and one of the busiest. Thousands of people walking on embattled tundra plants would damage them significantly. Therefore, in this Tundra Protection Zone, stay on the paved Tundra World Trail.

The best diversity of tundra plants along the trail occurs at the trailhead, the most sheltered place for low-angle, tripod-using, wait-for-the-miserable-wind-to-quit photography of flowers. Typical of this area are some larger

Toll Memorial

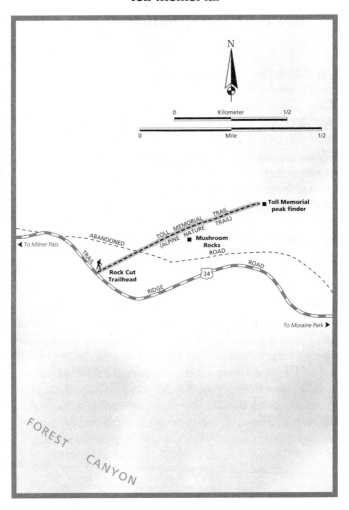

tundra species: purple fringe, sky pilot, bistort, and alpine sunflower.

For the first quarter mile, the edge of the asphalt is crowded by cushion plants pioneering the wind-scoured rock fields. Pink moss campion predominates, with white alpine sandwort also heroically struggling to bring life to the barren domain of the bitter wind. Watch for patterns of tundra flowers growing amid lines of jagged rocks (felsenmeer) heaved together and thrust up by the freezing and thawing of the ground.

The progress of this effort can be judged a short way up the trail, where an abandoned road dating from the construction of Trail Ridge Road comes in from the left. Quarry rock was transported along this road in the early 1930s. Although the twin ruts of truck tires are still obvious in the shape of the ground, the cushion plants have made equally obvious progress in covering the surface.

The path's beginning steepness distresses many motorists, who drive quickly and easily from oxygen-rich air at low altitude to thin air at high altitude. After the grade flattens, a spur path takes hikers to Mushroom Rocks, caprock formations unusual in this park. White feldspar that fractures easily into plates makes up most of the rock below caps of hard schist, more resistant to wind and temperature erosion.

Stark color contrast and mushroom shapes make the rocks very photogenic. Less obvious is the pattern of cushion plants standing out against an unusual background of white rock chips along the trail west of Mushroom Rocks.

The last half of the trail is relatively flat until the last scramble up a rock outcrop to the peak finder that memorializes Roger Toll, third park superintendent, who envisioned the building of Trail Ridge Road. The easier grade relieves the lungs, but does not help skin chilled by wind and low temperature and scorched by UV radiation. Appropriate clothing and sunscreen greatly enhance your enjoyment of the high-altitude tundra.

19
FALL RIVER PASS TO MILNER PASS

Type of hike: Shuttle.
Total distance: 4 miles.
Maps: Trails Illustrated; Fall River Pass USGS quad.
Highlights: Alpine tundra, easy downhill hike (4 miles), good views of Never Summer Range.
Wildlife: Mule deer, elk, ptarmigan, white-crowned sparrow.
Fall River Pass elevation: 11,796 feet.
Milner Pass elevation: 10,750 feet.

Finding the trailhead: Fall River Pass is located along Trail Ridge Road about midway between Estes Park and Grand Lake. Milner Pass is 4.2 miles west of Fall River Pass on Trail Ridge Road.

The hike: One of the easiest and most pleasant trails in Rocky Mountain National Park is relatively uncrowded because of logistical complications in arranging transportation at both ends of the trail. All downhill, a stroll along the 1918–1932 road route from Fall River Pass to Milner Pass follows a very easy grade. If you cannot work out a car shuttle to put wheels on both ends of the trail, the way back up to Fall River Pass from midway down at Forest Canyon Pass is not terribly steep.

Fall River Pass to Milner Pass

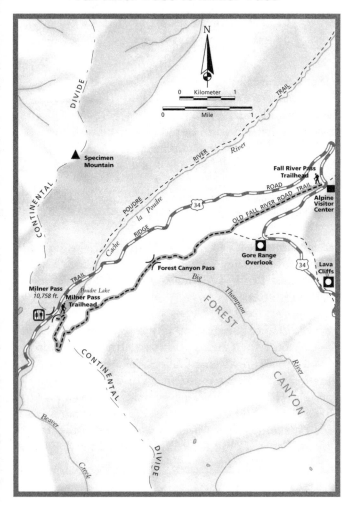

Abandoned when the present route of Trail Ridge Road was opened, the old route is an obvious path beginning across the road from the parking lot at Fall River Pass. Revegetation is still in its initial stage as the tundra cushion plants, primarily moss campion, pioneer the barren gravel once traveled by Model Ts. This is one of the best places in the national park to view the process of plant succession. The campion traps bits of windblown dirt under its many-branched stem, hoarding the soil until this reservoir of dirt can support plants less hardy than the pioneer campion. The campion shelters their seeds from fierce wind and provides food and moisture, and then the new plants establish themselves and crowd out the campion.

The old road offers a very fine view south to the Never Summer Range. The rusty red of the distant peaks accents a foreground of tundra flowers. Below Forest Canyon Pass, clumps of wind-abused Engelmann spruce provide a dramatic foreground for the rugged Never Summer Range.

Soon hikers traverse a forest where the same spruce species grows straight and tall. Bogs below melting snowbanks and occasional avalanche runs open the woods, giving light to masses of Indian paintbrush and other subalpine flowers. Where deep woods prevail, Jacob's ladder, with its ladderlike leaves and pale blue flowers, provides the ground cover.

A sign at a trail junction indicates that continuing straight takes hikers to a climb up Mount Ida. Make a sharp right turn to drop through gentle switchbacks to the Continental Divide at Milner Pass.

20
THE CRATER

Type of hike: Out-and-back.
Total distance: 2 miles.
Maps: Trails Illustrated; Fall River Pass USGS quad.
Highlights: Classic subalpine forest, good views of Never Summer Range from The Crater (1 mile), excellent wildflower display, wildlife.
Wildlife: Mule deer, elk, marmot, bighorn sheep.
Trailhead elevation: 10,750 feet.
The Crater elevation: 11,480 feet.

Finding the trailhead: Trailhead parking is located on the west side of Trail Ridge Road opposite the midpoint of Poudre Lake. Rest rooms and more parking are at the south end of the lake. The trail is closed during the lambing season (through early July).

The hike: Most people climbing the steep trail to The Crater on Specimen Mountain hope to see bighorn sheep. Their chances for success are good. Binoculars likely will be welcome, but the sheep may decide to throng 50 feet away or not show up at all.

Even without sheep, the trail compacts many fine experiences into a short length. The wet meadow at the base can be an explosion of subalpine wildflower color after the middle of the summer. The cool, damp forest

The Crater

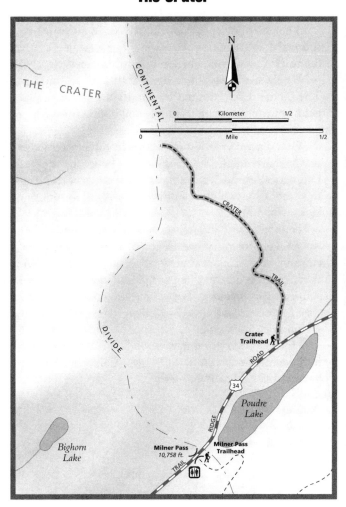

boasts dense stands of mature subalpine fir and Engelmann spruce, where deer are very common.

The wildflowers, particularly various paintbrush species, are outstanding at tree line. The view of the Never Summer Range from The Crater is excellent.

Be especially careful to tread lightly on the tundra at The Crater. Concentrated foot traffic here plus the funneling of wind through this low point of Specimen Mountain have kept the plant cover sparse.

Outcrops of volcanic rock covered by colorful lichens accent views of the Never Summer Range to the west. Dramatically eroded volcanic ash rather than a real crater, this spot is a wildly beautiful backdrop for morning bighorn sightings.

For the sake of the sheep and the other hikers who want to see them, it is vital not to stalk the sheep for a close-up view. Enjoy whatever opportunities for viewing the bighorn decide to offer, but do not stress the sheep by acting like a predator. The whole mountain is a special sheep preserve and closed to hiking during the lambing season in early summer.

Hiking on up Specimen beyond The Crater is always forbidden. You can climb left, toward Shipler Mountain, but stay out of The Crater itself.

21
LULU CITY

Type of hike: Out-and-back.
Total distance: 7.4 miles.
Maps: Trails Illustrated; Fall River Pass USGS quad.
Highlights: Shipler Mine (2.5 miles), Lulu City (3.7 miles).
Wildlife: Elk, mule deer, gray jay, red squirrel.
Colorado River Trailhead elevation: 9,010 feet.
Lulu City elevation: 9,360 feet.

Finding the trailhead: The Colorado River Trailhead is on the west side of Trail Ridge Road, 9.6 miles north of the Grand Lake entrance to Rocky Mountain National Park and 10.7 miles southwest of Fall River Pass.

The hike: Lulu City was never a city, and it was never a lulu. Lulu City was a vain hope that silver deposits in the Never Summer Range would be rich enough to exploit profitably. The streets laid out on paper in 1880 never passed more than the few buildings it took to serve 50 to 200 residents until the community's complete abandonment by 1884. These buildings are gone, and the few remaining logs and stone foundations and rusting bits of mining machinery are not obvious.

Lulu City

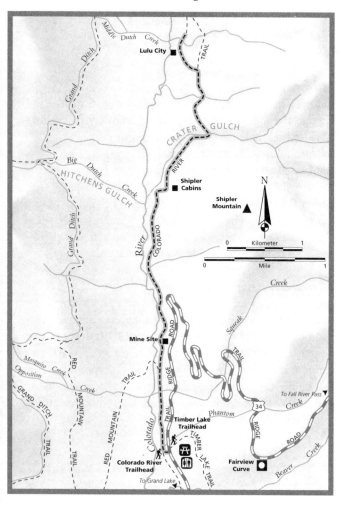

Distracted by the rich scenery, hikers often give no thought to the riches sought by Lulu City founders and residents. Even history enthusiasts usually are more impressed by the unbankable riches of wildflower color and jagged, snow-accented skyline than by the hopes of silver miners.

At 0.6 mile from the trailhead is the site of the old Phantom Valley guest ranch, where a trail to Red Mountain splits left from the trail to Lulu City and La Poudre Pass. The way to Lulu City continues fairly level along the Colorado River. Willows and other floodplain plants line the trail, and the workings of beavers are obvious. Human workings also appear in an 1880s mine site to the right of the trail beyond the split.

Shipler Mine, at 2.5 miles, preceded Lulu City and lasted until 1914. It likely was no more successful at producing silver, but Joe Shipler loved the land and hung on despite lack of riches, a common story even today in Grand County. He built his first sod-roofed cabin in 1876 and over the years managed to peck 100 yards into the granite of Shipler Mountain. Very lucky hikers may see mountain sheep amid the rubble of Shipler's mining efforts. (Stay out of all old mines; they are not safe.)

Passing on a level grade beyond the cabins, the trail follows a stage road that ran to Lulu City before heading northwest over Thunder Pass to Walden, Colorado. When at last the trail climbs above the valley floor, the shade of subalpine forest through which you walk is welcome. The trail forks at a junction 3.5 miles from the trailhead. The right-hand fork goes to the eroded volcanic rock of Little Yellowstone Canyon and La Poudre Pass. The left-hand fork heads back downhill through switchbacks for about 0.2 mile to the meadow that contained Lulu City. The Thunder Pass Trail continues through the meadow and past a steep connecting trail up to the La Poudre Pass Trail.

22
BIG MEADOWS

Type of hike: Loop.
Total distance: 7 miles.
Maps: Trails Illustrated; Grand Lake USGS quad.
Highlights: Circle hike, Big Meadows (1.8 miles), log building ruins in Big Meadows.
Wildlife: Mule deer, elk, red squirrel, mountain chickadee.
Green Mountain Trailhead elevation: 8,794 feet.
Big Meadows elevation: 9,400 feet.

Finding the trailhead: The Onahu Creek and Green Mountain trailheads are 0.6 mile apart and are well marked along Trail Ridge Road, about 3 miles north of the Grand Lake entrance to Rocky Mountain National Park and 17 miles southwest of Fall River Pass.

The hike: Some folks in turn-of-the-twentieth-century Grand Lake thought Sam Stone was crazy. Perhaps he would seem less so today, since Colorado has attracted a population with a higher-than-average percentage of eccentrics. In any case, Sam tried to produce hay in marshy Big Meadows, which he hauled by wagon down what now is the Green Mountain Trail.

How well his idea worked is difficult to determine because he gave it up when a woman spiritualist informed him that she had divined the presence of gold in Paradise

Big Meadows

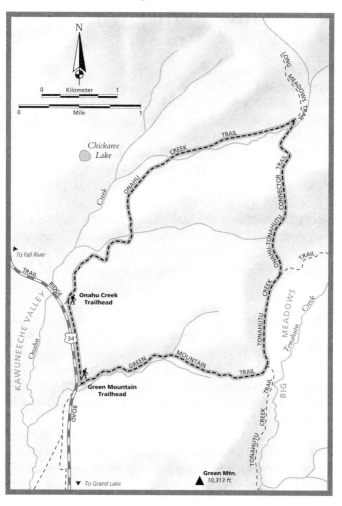

Park on Rocky Mountain National Park's southern boundary. Together they went off to strike it rich, but no sign of them or gold can be found in Paradise Park today. The ruins of Sam's log cabin and barn, however, still remain in Big Meadows.

Hiking northeast on the Green Mountain Trail, you will find that the approach to Sam's old ranch is relatively wide, free of rocks, and gentle of grade. The trail follows a well-watered gully that is full of a greater than usual variety of plants. In winter, good snow accumulation and a comparatively easy grade make this an excellent trail for ski touring and snowshoeing.

At Big Meadows, head left (north) along the Tonahutu Creek Trail to investigate the remains of Sam's log buildings. Mount Ida is obvious to the north, its left slope seemingly gentle, its right a steep drop-off. Beaver ponds and marsh dominate the foreground. The trail avoids the wet areas, skirting Big Meadows just inside the forest edge.

Continue north to where a path branches steeply left from the Tonahutu Creek Trail, almost a mile from the Green Mountain Trail. Ascend the left branch over a ridge to the Onahu Creek drainage. A clear trail crosses Onahu Creek on a bridge and follows the creek southwest through spruce and fir, lodgepole pine, aspen, and willows down to Trail Ridge Road. A 0.6-mile trail through the woods parallels the road back to your car at Green Mountain Trailhead.

23
COYOTE VALLEY

Type of hike: Out-and-back.
Total distance: 1.6 miles.
Maps: Trails Illustrated; Grand Lake USGS quad.
Highlights: Colorado River, views of Never Summer Range, wildlife.
Wildlife: Elk, mule deer, moose, coyote, black-billed magpie.
Coyote Valley Trailhead elevation: 8,846 feet.

Finding the trailhead: Coyote Valley Trailhead is on the west side of Trail Ridge Road, 6.1 miles north of the Grand Lake entrance to Rocky Mountain National Park and 14.2 miles southwest of Fall River Pass.

The hike: Of the 297 bridges that carry hikers over streams in Rocky Mountain National Park, the bridge at the beginning of the Coyote Valley Trail must be the most elaborate, a humbler version of the magnificent Carriage Path bridges in Acadia National Park. This structure across the Colorado River leads to a wheelchair-accessible path along the level floodplain. Many benches and signs help visitors to appreciate and understand the riverside environment on the west side of Rocky Mountain National Park. Broad loops, detours, and cul-de-sacs provide variety in hiking to the trail's end and back.

Coyote Valley

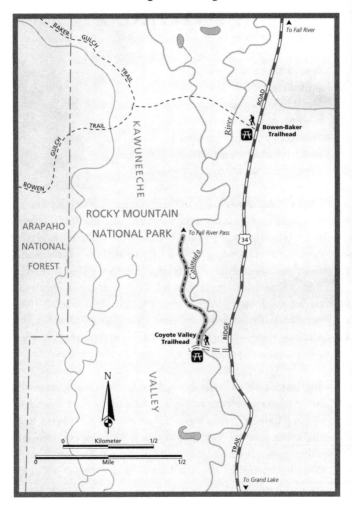

24
ADAMS FALLS

Type of hike: Out-and-back.
Total distance: 0.6 mile.
Maps: Trails Illustrated; Shadow Mountain USGS quad.
Highlights: Adams Falls (0.3 mile).
Wildlife: Gray jay, water ouzel, mountain chickadee.
East Inlet Trailhead elevation: 8,391 feet.
Adams Falls elevation: 8,470 feet.

Finding the trailhead: East Inlet Trailhead is at the end of
Tunnel Road (Colorado Highway 278). Take CO 278 east
from US Highway 34 at the village of Grand Lake. After
one-third mile, take the left fork to bypass the town and
head directly to Adams Tunnel, a link in the Colorado–Big
Thompson Irrigation Project. Follow more than 2 miles of
paved road to the West Portal of Adams Tunnel. (The
west end of the tunnel is at the East Inlet to Grand Lake,
a minor point of confusion.) At the West Portal, bear left
on the unpaved road to the trailhead parking area.

The hike: The easy walk to Adams Falls rises gradually
amid lodgepole pines and glacially deposited boulders.
Adams Falls is within a gorge that evidently follows a geo-
logic crack formed during the uplift of the Rockies and
subsequently altered by glacial scouring and water erosion.
Splashing through this defile, East Inlet throws up much

Adams Falls

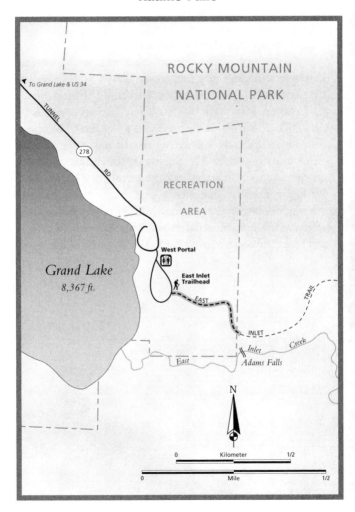

spray, which can form rainbows around the falls. To see a rainbow, you must have the sun behind you as you look at the water droplets in the air.

Rocks around Adams Falls are smooth, steep, and often wet, all of which contribute to treacherous footing. Parents should take care that their children do not slip into the stream and get washed over the brink. Although the falls make a lovely photo subject, we have exposed more film at Adams Falls on the rescue of a woman who slipped on the slick rocks and broke her arm falling to the ground, never touching the water. She remained conscious and in courageous spirits throughout the rescue on a wheeled litter. Despite the relative closeness of the road and comparative gentleness of the terrain, her extraction from the wilderness edge seemed long and complicated, inspiring us to be cautious when we hike deep into the wilderness.

Winter Trails

Winter in the park is not exactly quiet. When the wind does not drown the chatter of chickadees, nuthatches, and squirrels, the rhythmic swish of cross-country skis or the creak-crunch of snowshoes lulls backcountry travelers. Although few of its wildlife inhabitants truly hibernate, the park itself seems peacefully drowsy, if not actually asleep.

Winter visitors should wake up to the beauty and fun available for snatching on short days. Visitors should also wake up to the potential hazards of winter, which are more intimidating than in the gentle Rocky Mountain wilderness of summer. In winter, you do not have to worry about lightning, but snow, wind, cold, and ice add the need for even greater caution than in summer.

We would not mention that ice is slick, except that we have experienced some really dumb and potentially fatal falls by dreamily overlooking this seemingly obvious reality. Ice carved the beauty of Rocky Mountain National Park, and enough ice remains to make winter footing hazardous for the incautious. Frozen waterfalls are particularly dangerous, but stream courses that make good winter routes also occasionally have slick spots barely covered by snow or swept bare by wind.

Lake ice can be thin near inlets and outlets. Hikers, snowshoers, and skiers should travel far apart to lessen the stress on the ice and to make aid available to the unlucky one (hopefully just one) who ends up in frigid water.

Winter Overview Map

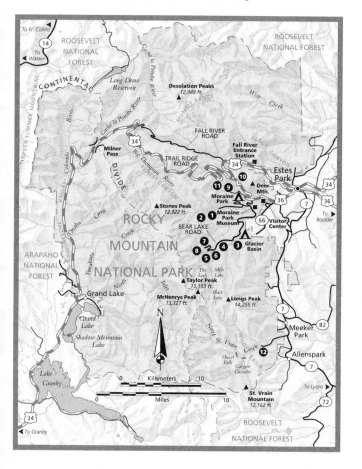

Enos Mills, Father of Rocky Mountain National Park, wrote, "In winter I discovered solitude, boiled down, refined, and twenty-two carat." Despite this praise, traveling alone in the backcountry in winter is a bad idea. Sharing the glories of the winter backcountry with a companion increases the enjoyment of those joys for everyone, and companions can provide help in case of trouble.

This is especially true of getting caught and buried by an avalanche. Chances of survival decrease by 50 percent after burial for a half hour; the help available at the time of the avalanche is likely to be the only help that will matter. The National Park Service recommends that each member of the winter travel group carry a light shovel in avalanche country. Lacking a shovel, companions can dig effectively with skis and snowshoes. Of course, rescuers should dig with all possible speed, but watch out for subsequent slides. Travel far apart when crossing potential avalanche areas to reduce chances that more than one person can be hit.

Most winter travelers injured or killed by avalanches trigger the slides themselves. You can avoid loosening unstable masses of snow by not crossing open slopes that have a pitch of 30 to 45 degrees, where avalanches most frequently occur.

This avoidance is easier than might seem likely in the steep terrain of Rocky Mountain National Park. With some disconcerting exceptions, the most dangerous places are the glacier-carved bowls and cliffs along the Continental Divide where wind deposits huge amounts of snow swept from the tundra. Ridges that extend east and west from the Continental Divide can carry the zone of danger to the vicinity of some popular backcountry travel routes. Most valleys and forests are safe, but even these slide occasionally.

Just as lightning has repeated strike areas in summer, avalanches tend to plague danger zones repeatedly in winter. Broad vertical bands of treeless avalanche runs are easy to spot. Somewhat more subtle are broken small trees and branches. A hollow sound under snowshoes or skis is not reassuring, especially on the east and north sides of ridges where wind tends to drop snow. Snowballs rolling down the slope from your feet is a bad sign. Cracks opening and lengthening is a very bad sign of slab avalanche, calling for immediate, cautious departure from the area.

If you trigger an avalanche, ditch your pack, ski poles, and skis or snowshoes and try to use a swimming motion to stay atop the snow. If you go under, protect your nose and mouth with your hands to preserve a breathing space.

By definition, park visitors are not around the park all the time and therefore may not be aware of previous weather conditions that increase avalanche hazards. Because there are no obvious signs of this danger, it is a good idea to check with park staff about recent weather history before venturing into potential avalanche areas, especially those not detailed in this book. Recent snowstorms account for 80 percent of avalanches. The gloriously clear and even windless day may be dangerously deceptive to the person who was not present to experience the previous day's howling blizzard. Long periods of cold temperatures can increase the period of instability leading to avalanches.

Returning to statements of deep profundity, temperatures tend to be cold in winter. To your body, cold and wind are pretty much the same thing, and bitter winds are frequent in Rocky Mountain National Park. Winds of 100 miles per hour are not unusual. The difference between pleasant winter briskness on the lowlands and killing windy cold on the heights can be extreme.

Always carry more clothing than you think you will need. Proving that the mind is the first thing to go when the body tires of struggling through snow, jackets sometimes remain in packs while their owners are at least very uncomfortable and perhaps dying from the cold. Remember to add and subtract the layers of clothing you carry. At least two sets of gloves are light, easy insurance against one pair becoming useless after getting wet. Heavy boots are more appropriate in winter than in summer.

Colorado has the nation's highest rate of skin cancer due to the state's high altitude and resulting thin air and low protection from solar radiation. The danger of solar radiation causing painful sunburn, aging skin, and possibly fatal cancer is even greater in cold winter than warm summer. The angle of sunlight is lower in winter, which cuts down on exposure to radiation, but the weather tends to be clearer all day in winter than in summer, reducing the shield of clouds. Snow reflects most of the solar radiation that hits it, almost doubling the dose your skin receives and directing that radiation to parts of your face that normally are shaded from direct sun and thus unprotected by the skin's natural defenses.

Every day, eliminate this danger by applying sunscreen with a high sun protection factor. This is the simplest, easiest, and most beneficial safety action you can take while enjoying the beautiful solitude of winter trails in Rocky Mountain National Park.

WINTER TRAIL 1
WINTER HIKE TO CUB LAKE

Type of hike: Out-and-back.
Total distance: 4.6 miles.
Maps: Trails Illustrated; McHenrys Peak and Longs Peak USGS quads.
Highlights: Ice patterns, wildlife, Cub Lake (2.3 miles).
Wildlife: Mule deer, elk, coyote.
Trailhead elevation: 8,080 feet.
Cub Lake elevation: 8,620 feet.

Finding the trailhead: From the Beaver Meadows entrance to Rocky Mountain National Park, follow Bear Lake Road 1.2 miles and turn right toward Moraine Park Campground. Follow the signs for 2.2 miles to the Cub Lake Trailhead.

The trip: Famous in summer for flowers, butterflies, and birds, the Cub Lake Trail presents a different but still fascinating face in winter. The lushness of summer falls away, leaving a scene dominated by angular patterns, bold shapes, and subdued tones rather than individual splashes of brightly colored flora and fauna that attract attention in warm months.

For more than a mile, the trail is mostly flat and easy, usually with little snow. The last mile is steeper. Ice or sections of deep snow can make the way difficult, requiring snowshoes or skis.

Winter Hike to Cub Lake

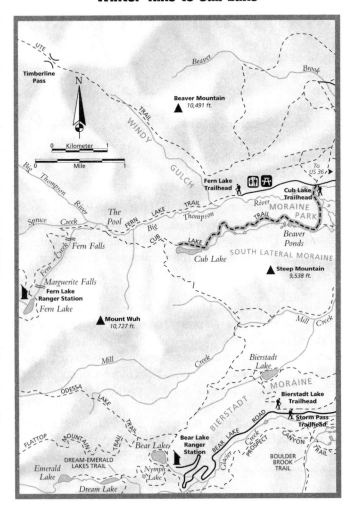

Naked willows and low water make the banks of the Big Thompson River near the trailhead more sharply defined. Because few large boulders break up the flow of this part of the river, the river itself actually is more interesting in winter where water undercuts patterns of ice ledges.

Where the trail leaves thickets and meadows behind as it enters ponderosa pine and Douglas-fir woods, watch for large boulders perched on broad slabs of rock. These are glacial erratics, dropped when the most recent ice sheet melted some 10,000 years ago. In the background is the South Lateral Moraine, the long, dark ridge for which Moraine Park is named.

If snow does not lighten the trees on the north slope, the moraine in winter can be a dark, simple background for photos of the massive granite erratics. Shoot south to emphasize their bold shapes by backlighting them with a halolike rim of light around them, contrasting with the dark background.

Although spotting elk, deer, or coyotes is extremely likely anywhere along the first part of the trail, where the path bends west may be the most productive place to watch, especially in late afternoon. Crouching behind a good-sized erratic will make you somewhat less conspicuous and a good deal more patient if you use the rock as protection from the wind.

At the lake, the best scenic shot is from east shore, looking toward Stones Peak. Find some interesting fallen tree or rocks as foreground. A short telephoto will make the peak more impressive.

WINTER TRAIL 2
THE POOL IN WINTER

Type of hike: Out-and-back.
Total distance: 5 miles.
Maps: Trails Illustrated; McHenrys Peak USGS quad.
Highlights: Arch Rocks (2 miles), The Pool (2.5 miles).
Wildlife: Mule deer, elk, red squirrel, mountain chickadee.
Trailhead elevation: 8,155 feet.
The Pool elevation: 8,320 feet.

Finding the trailhead: From the Beaver Meadows entrance to Rocky Mountain National Park, drive 1.2 miles along Bear Lake Road and turn right toward Moraine Park Campground. Follow the signs for 2.3 miles to a road closure just beyond Cub Lake Trailhead.

The trip: The Pool is a water pocket in the Big Thompson River just below its confluence with Spruce and Fern Creeks. The spot is marked by a bridge across the Big Thompson and is an easy hike at nearly all times of the year. Because the trail is on a south-facing slope, the snow cover is relatively slight or absent for most of the winter.

The winter trail begins as 0.8 mile of unpaved, closed road that is open in summer. Most of the closed road passes through stands of quaking aspen. The white aspen trunks are heavily textured with black scars caused by elk stripping off the bark for winter food. You may find elk feeding among these aspen stands.

The Pool in Winter

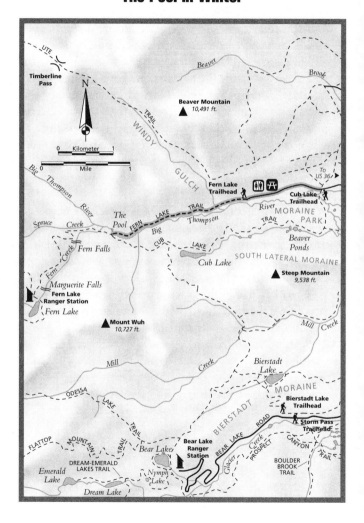

At Fern Lake Trail, the route narrows to a trail surrounded by narrowleaf cottonwood, not a particularly common tree at this elevation. The furrowed cottonwood bark is interesting in the low angle of slanting winter light.

For young children, beaver-cut aspen stumps along the trail make a worthwhile destination about a mile short of The Pool. This playground designed by flat-tailed engineers can fascinate kids for a long time—two or three minutes. Arch Rocks, the very large boulders among which the trail winds along the river, probably were not dropped by retreating glaciers but rather fell from the cliffs above as a result of freezing and thawing water wedging them off.

Beyond Arch Rocks, The Pool is a wide spot where a bridge crosses the Big Thompson River. Of course many pools decorate the length of the Big Thompson River, but this cliff-bound pool is a bit more spectacular than most, even when winter has quieted its whirling torrent.

The Pool gained its particular notoriety through history rather than spectacle. In 1889 a university biological expedition in Moraine Park included Frederick Funston. Although Funston would eventually go on to become a notable general in the Spanish-American War, his virtues of command cut no ice with the students on the expedition when he fell into the river. They named the spot Funston Pool, which the U.S. Board of Geological Names shortened to The Pool in 1932.

WINTER TRAIL 3
SKIING TO SPRAGUE LAKE

Type of trip: Loop.
Total distance: 3 miles.
Maps: Trails Illustrated; Longs Peak USGS quad.
Highlights: Easy trail, Sprague Lake (1.5 miles).
Wildlife: Mule deer, Steller's jay.
Glacier Basin Campground Trailhead elevation: 8,590 feet.
Sprague Lake elevation: 8,710 feet.

Finding the trailhead: From the Beaver Meadows entrance to Rocky Mountain National Park, drive about 5 miles along the Bear Lake Road to the well-marked entrance to Glacier Basin Campground. Parking is across Bear Lake Road from the campground's entrance.

The trip: This may be the most ideal ski trip for beginners on the east side of Rocky Mountain National Park. Three miles round-trip over gentle terrain, the route between Glacier Basin Campground and Sprague Lake usually holds enough snow to cover rocks and logs. During warm spells, though, it could be patchy and icy in some sections, calling for ski removal and a short walk.

This is an excellent short trip for both novice and experienced cross-country skiers or snowshoers. The trail passes through open meadow, woods, streamside, and lakeshore. Although short in distance, the trip may take longer than expected due to frequent stops to enjoy the scenery.

Skiing to Sprague Lake

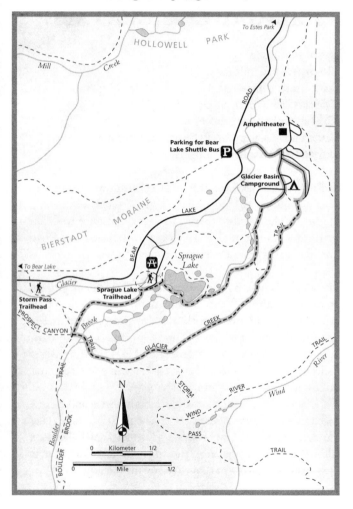

The road into Glacier Basin Campground is blocked at Bear Lake Road in winter. Just beyond the barrier, skiers and snowshoers cross the bridge over Glacier Creek.

Continue up the campground road into a broad meadow with magnificent views of the Front Range. On the opposite side of the meadow are campground C and D Loops. Bear to the left and enter C Loop to campsite 42. From here follow the access path to the Glacier Creek Trail to Storm Pass. Beyond the campsites, brightly colored tags nailed to the trees mark the trail to Sprague Lake. A short way up this trail, the tags become difficult to spot and another trail heads downhill to the right. A sign at this junction indicates the trail to the right goes to Sprague Lake, but do not take this trail. Instead, continue uphill to the left toward Storm Pass. Soon you will spot the bright markers in the trees again. Follow the markers for just over a mile through pleasant woods to a junction where five trails come together. At this somewhat baffling maze, make a sharp right turn (still following the trail markers) for an easy, but exciting ski run to a picnic area at Sprague Lake.

Bear right across the picnic area to a bridge crossing a pond at the west end of Sprague Lake. Follow the trail around the southern shore (to the right). The trip's best photos are from the eastern shore of Sprague Lake. (For more photo opportunities explore a bit further along the lake shore beyond where the marked trail departs along a brook back to Glacier Basin Campground.) From the lake's outlet on the east shore, follow trail markers back to D Loop in Glacier Basin Campground.

WINTER TRAIL 4
SKIING FROM GLACIER
GORGE JUNCTION TO
SPRAGUE LAKE

Type of trip: Shuttle.
Total distance: 3 miles.
Maps: Trails Illustrated; McHenrys Peak and Longs Peak USGS quads.
Highlights: Downhill for 3 miles.
Wildlife: Red squirrel, mountain chickadee, snowshoe hare.
Glacier Gorge Junction elevation: 9,230 feet.
Sprague Lake elevation: 8,710 feet.

Finding the trailhead: Glacier Gorge Junction is a small parking lot within a switchback in Bear Lake Road 8.5 miles from Rocky Mountain National Park's Beaver Meadows entrance.

The Sprague Lake picnic area is about 6.3 miles along Bear Lake Road from Highway 36 west of the Beaver Meadows entrance to Rocky Mountain National Park. A sign indicates a turn to the left from Bear Lake Road.

The trip: Little used by hikers in summer, the trail between Glacier Gorge Junction and Sprague Lake is a delightful ski trip when there is enough snow to cover rocks and logs. To take advantage of this one-way downhill route, skiers need to leave cars at Sprague Lake and Glacier Gorge

Skiing from Glacier Gorge Junction to Sprague Lake

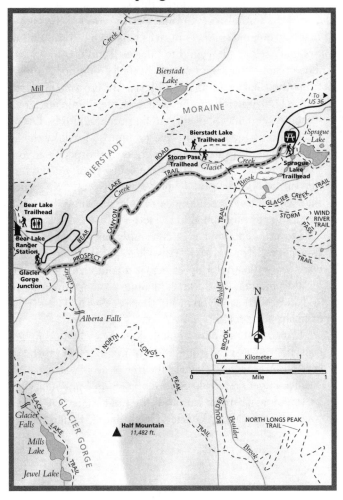

Junction. The park's Bear Lake shuttle does not operate in winter.

The summer trail along the south side of Glacier Creek is not always obvious when covered by snow. Brightly colored markers in trees help to mark the trail to Sprague Lake and beyond to Glacier Basin Campground. The greatest chance for error is at the beginning. Turn left from the Glacier Gorge Trail just after crossing the first bridge. Do not follow the Glacier Creek drainage; cross the creek and stay above it, circling rock outcrops. Dropping too low too soon will lead to a mess of willow thickets and other very frustrating barriers in Prospect Canyon.

The route traverses above the valley floor, encountering various beaver ponds. These supply water to shrubs that will be a severe nuisance to skiers or snowshoers, so strive to keep the ponds to the left.

Do not keep your eyes constantly on your ski tips or snowshoes. Not only will eyes glued to the ground cause you to miss many lovely scenes, you could also miss your guiding markers in the trees. Failing to look up, around, and ahead may land you in a bothersome natural cu-de-sac of bushes and rocks.

In any case, you are unlikely to stray too far from the trail. For most of the route, the terrain guides you through very pleasant woods. Beyond the beaver pond maze, nearly 3 miles of gentle terrain continue down to Sprague Lake.

Enjoy as abstract sculpture the bold shapes of snow-covered rocks along Glacier Creek and Boulder Brook.

The big snows that open this route to skiers and snow-shoers can also balance delicate piles of snow on shrub branches. If you get on the trail before the wind picks up, you may encounter some of these snow forms, which make interesting photos.

Avalanche risk is slight along this route, but skiers and snowshoers do face a couple of stream crossings. Test the ice with a ski pole to make sure that it is strong enough to bear your weight. If in doubt, remove skis or snowshoes and find a way across on rocks and logs.

WINTER TRAIL 5
LOCH VALE

Type of trip: Out-and-back.
Total distance: 4.6 miles.
Maps: Trails Illustrated; McHenrys Peak USGS quad.
Highlights: Loch Vale (1.5 miles), The Loch (2.3 miles).
Wildlife: Mountain chickadee, snowshoe hare, red squirrel, gray jay.
Glacier Gorge Junction elevation: 9,230 feet.
The Loch elevation: 10,180 feet.

Finding the trailhead: From the Park's Beaver Meadows entrance, follow Bear Lake Road 8.3 miles to Glacier Gorge Junction, a small parking lot within a switchback.

The trip: One of the most popular trails in Rocky Mountain National Park in the summer, the path from the Glacier Gorge Trailhead to Alberta Falls is pleasant for winter travelers. But the frozen falls are probably less interesting than in the summer, and portions of the trail beyond often are swept clear of snow by the wind. Drifts in other areas may be hip deep. A pattern of on again, off again with snowshoes or skis would be likely on this slope.

However, there is a more snowy route on the northwest side of Glacier Knobs that also is a bit steeper but within the abilities of snowshoers or advanced beginning skiers. After crossing the second bridge on the Alberta Falls Trail (about a quarter mile from the trailhead), turn

Loch Vale

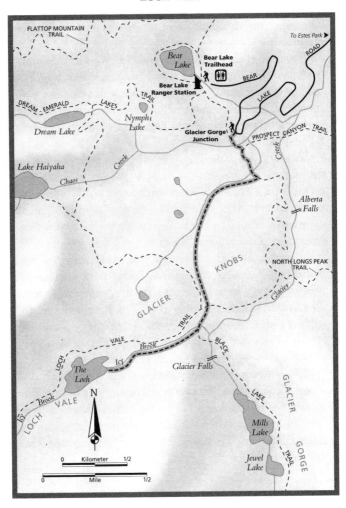

right up a small valley, which is mostly hidden by trees. Sometimes you can follow tracks of previous parties up a somewhat terraced landscape, altered in places by beaver engineering.

Even in this protected gorge, the wind sometimes howls, raising clouds of snow. You are headed in a southerly direction, so you will be facing into whatever sun there is. Your companions silhouetted against the backlit clouds of blowing snow can make a very dramatic photo. A lens hood will help.

At the Loch Vale–Glacier Gorge trail junction, ignore the summer route up Loch Vale, which is steep and windswept. Head left a short way toward Mills Lake as far as Icy Brook, then bear right up the streambed for a snowier route to The Loch. Try to stay to the right of the stream; ice along the banks sometimes is undercut by dark, frigid water. Plunging through here could dampen your whole trip. The large spruces and firs in the stream course present lovely forms and textures when clothed in snow. The risk of avalanche along the valley floor is slight, but caution is always necessary, especially after high winds following a snowstorm. This typical pattern may set up unstable snow slopes in atypical locations.

Classic views of Taylor Peak and the Cathedral Wall above The Loch can be even more striking in winter than in summer, but the island in the lake that provides a highlight in summer is less visible in winter. Wind-sculpted limber pines on the lakeshore provide interesting foreground shapes for the view of Taylor Peak.

WINTER TRAIL 6
WINTER IN GLACIER GORGE

Type of trip: Out-and-back.
Total distance: 8.4 miles.
Maps: Trails Illustrated; McHenrys Peak USGS quad.
Highlights: Mills Lake (2.1 miles), Black Lake (4.2 miles).
Wildlife: Gray jay, snowshoe hare.
Glacier Gorge Junction elevation: 9,230 feet.
Mills Lake elevation: 9,940 feet.
Black Lake elevation: 10,620 feet.

Finding the trailhead: Glacier Gorge Junction is a small parking lot within a switchback on Bear Lake Road, 8.5 miles from Rocky Mountain National Park's Beaver Meadows entrance.

The trip: Trekking to Black Lake is somewhat tiring on a single short winter day. Spring storms may open Black Lake to easier access as days lengthen through April.

The risk of avalanches for winter travelers who ascend along the valley floor of Glacier Gorge is low enough to be acceptable, but caution always is appropriate, especially beyond Mills Lake.

The beginning of the summer trail to Glacier Gorge usually has poor snow conditions, so cut to the right just after the second bridge on the trail to ascend a snowier valley northwest of Glacier Knobs. Where the trail splits to Loch Vale and Glacier Gorge, head left to cross Icy

Winter in Glacier Gorge

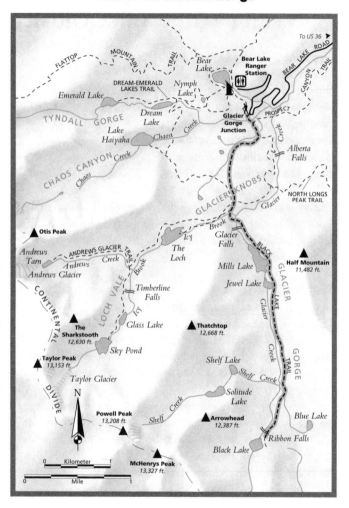

Brook on a bridge and follow the summer trail into Glacier Gorge.

Especially in winter, when the sun is farther south, the light on Longs Peak above Mills Lake is more dramatic in the afternoon. Shapes of interesting trees or rocks against expanses of ice make a frozen lake surface more interesting. However, on the way to Black Lake, photograph Longs Peak at Mills Lake in the morning in case storm or wind hide the peaks behind snow on your way back. But hope to reshoot in the afternoon.

Early in the day is the time to photograph McHenry's Peak, which rises directly from Black Lake. Probably the best views of McHenry's will be from farther away, down Glacier Gorge from Black Lake. Put your silhouetted companions, snow-covered rocks, and trees in the foreground. Ice climbers may be pursuing their chilly joys on frozen splashes that drape the cliffs above Black Lake. Take lunch on the lip of rock that contains the lake, and look back down Glacier Gorge to note the obvious U-shape of the valley profile, typical of glaciated mountain valleys.

WINTER TRAIL 7
BEAR LAKE TO
HOLLOWELL PARK

Type of trip: Shuttle.
Total distance: 4.5 miles.
Maps: Trails Illustrated; McHenrys Peak and Longs Peak USGS quads.
Highlights: Bierstadt Lake (1.6 miles), delightful woodland trail.
Wildlife: Gray jay, snowshoe hare
Bear Lake Trailhead elevation: 9,475 feet.
High point: 9,730 feet.

Finding the trailhead: Hollowell Park is 3.5 miles from the Beaver Meadows entrance to the national park. Bear Lake is 5.5 miles farther at the end of the road.

The trip: This trail leads to Bierstadt Lake, a popular destination for backcountry travelers in Rocky Mountain National Park in both winter and summer. Frequently during the winter and spring, snowshoes or skis must be carried over some relatively snowless sections when hikers are traveling beyond the lake to meet Bear Lake Road in Hollowell Park.

Bright markers delineate the 4.5-mile route from the Bear Lake parking lot to Hollowell Park. Markers also lead to an alternative destination at the summer parking

Bear Lake to Hollowell Park

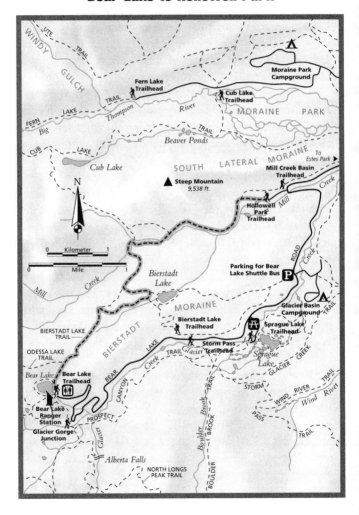

area for the Bear Lake Shuttle. Begin with a short, steep climb to the trail's high point, about 0.5 mile from Bear Lake. Thereafter the route is downhill for the remaining 4 miles. At the high point the Odessa Lake Trail heads left from the Bierstadt Lake Trail. The National Park Service considers the trail to Odessa Gorge to be avalanche prone.

Continuing on the Bierstadt Lake Trail, be aware that the initial south-facing section through the aspen on the side of boulder-strewn Bierstadt Moraine might not have enough snow to permit snowshoeing or skiing across windswept areas.

Snow conditions generally improve on the broad, gentle top of the moraine. Skiing down a very slight grade amid the lodgepole pine is delightful; the trail in winter often seems more pleasant and interesting than in summer. The repetitive lodgepole trunks form interesting straight line patterns emphasized by the snow.

After a mile of effortless kick-and-glide through the lodgepoles, skiers can detour right to views of Longs Peak across Bierstadt Lake. As in summer, there are no landmarks, and snow may cover the trail signs that guide hikers. However, there probably will be tracks of previous travelers in the snow, and the lake is not hard to find.

Beyond Bierstadt Lake toward Hollowell Park, the trail steepens considerably as it drops through denser north-slope forest along an old logging road. This mile can be challenging for skiers, especially if snow conditions are less than ideal. Be careful; try to maintain a slow, controlled speed to lessen the impact of falls occasioned by protruding rocks or sharp turns.

At Mill Creek, a bridge marks the end of the steepest section of trail. The trail descends past old beaver workings to the broad meadow of Hollowell Park. On a sunnier south-facing slope, the snow frequently does not survive. The last mile out to a car left at the trailhead on the drive up to Bear Lake often involves carrying the skis or snowshoes.

WINTER TRAIL 8
SKIING TO EMERALD LAKE

Type of trip: Out-and-back.
Total distance: 3.6 miles.
Maps: Trails Illustrated; McHenrys Peak USGS quad.
Highlights: Nymph Lake (0.5 mile), Dream Lake (1.1 miles), Emerald Lake (1.8 miles), wind-shaped limber pines at the lakes.
Wildlife: Gray jay, Clark's nutcracker, mountain chickadee, red squirrel.
Bear Lake elevation: 9,475 feet.
Emerald Lake elevation: 10,080 feet.

Finding the trailhead: From the park's Beaver Meadows entrance, follow Bear Lake Road 9 miles to its end at the Bear Lake Trailhead.

The trip: The most popular hike in the national park during the summer, the lakes above Bear Lake also attract many wilderness visitors in the winter. Using snowshoes or cross-country skis, park visitors find a winter world that is significantly different from summer in the same area.

Visually, the winter woods are cleaner and simpler, with snow covering the natural forest litter such as dead branches and needles. Snow covers intricate details (rocks, leaves, twigs, and bushes), emphasizing the bold, simple shapes of large branches, rocks, and trees.

Skiing to Emerald Lake

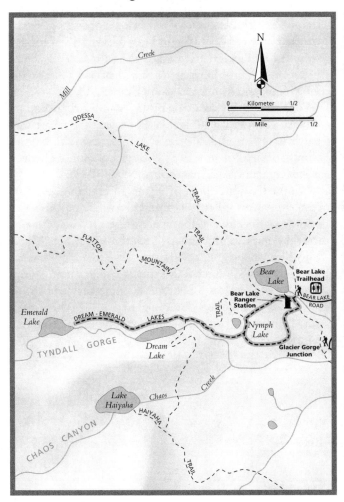

Avalanches are no threat on the leisurely half mile to Nymph Lake. Beyond to Dream and Emerald Lakes, the danger is slight, but caution is always a good policy, particularly between Nymph and Dream Lakes. (By contrast, there is more danger from avalanche on the trail between Dream and Haiyaha Lakes, a good reason to take the more popular trail from Dream to Emerald Lake.)

When snow is adequate on the south-facing summer trail to Nymph Lake, this is the best route. If there are bare patches on this trail, a steeper and less scenic alternative climbs from the west side of Bear Lake through deep woods on a north-facing slope to Nymph Lake.

From the west shore of Nymph Lake, an easy route climbs a narrow valley to Dream Lake which probably will be adequately frozen to support skiers or snowshoers, though some caution is advisable at the outlet. The firmest ice will be along the lake's south (left) edge. If there are tracks marking firm ice across the lake, follow them. From the west end of Dream Lake, head up the left side of Tyndall Creek Valley for a few hundred yards. Where the grade flattens, cut to the right through trees and continue on to Emerald Lake.

WINTER TRAIL 9
UPPER BEAVER MEADOWS IN WINTER

Type of trip: Loop.
Total distance: 3.5 miles.
Maps: Trails Illustrated; McHenrys Peak USGS quad.
Highlights: Elk exclosure to test effect of grazing (1.6 miles), glacial geology.
Wildlife: Mule deer, elk, black-billed magpie, raven.
Winter Beaver Meadows Trailhead elevation: 8,302 feet.
Upper Beaver Meadows Summer Trailhead elevation: 8,440 feet.

Finding the trailhead: The closed road into Upper Beaver Meadows begins on US 36 at a major bend 0.6 mile west of the Beaver Meadows entrance to Rocky Mountain National Park. Park in a turnout across US 36 from the trailhead.

The trip: This easy winter trail offers the option of a 3-mile hike with a canine companion. The out-and-back hike follows the closed road, which winds north of the creek. Hiking with leashed dogs is permitted for 1.5 miles to the road's end at the summer trailhead. Keeping dogs leashed is essential so that park managers will continue to allow hiking with dogs on closed roads.

The meadows are thick with elk and deer, which many

Upper Beaver Meadows in Winter

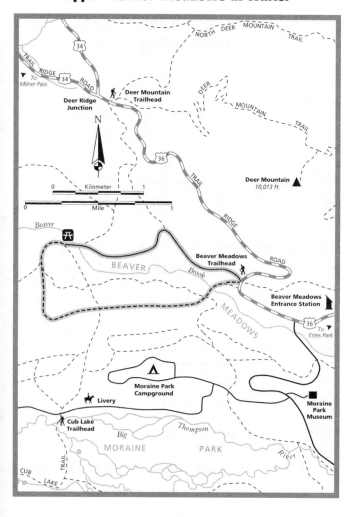

unleashed dogs would chase. During rut, mule deer bucks are likely to gore dogs that annoy them, resulting in very serious injury. Chasing wildlife is the cardinal sin that dogs can commit in a national park, although the deer and elk pay no more attention to leashed dogs than to human hikers. With their vastly superior senses of smell and hearing, leashed dogs may show you wild animals that you otherwise would have overlooked.

Dogs are not permitted on the trail beyond the end of the road. Hikers with dogs must return along the closed road.

To hike the loop route without dogs, follow a trail that leaves the road to head left just inside the road barricade near US 36. This trail, used mainly by horse riders in the summer, circles clockwise to the summer trailhead at the west end of the road, which leads back to the winter trailhead.

The long, forested ridge defining the south edge of Beaver Meadows is a moraine, a pile of rocks dropped by the melting ice of a glacier between 10,000 and 20,000 years ago. The trailhead sits more or less on the remnants of a moraine dumped by a larger glacier about 100,000 years earlier (a little more obvious directly east across the highway). Obviously, the younger moraine is much bigger. Many millennia of erosion of the older moraine accounts for much of the difference in height.

You are likely to see beavers in many places in the national park but not in Beaver Meadows. Presumably, these large rodents lived here in the late 1800s when homesteaders turned the meadows into irrigated hay fields. In previous centuries, Beaver Meadows was a favored summer campsite for Native Americans, and deadly battles between warring tribes reputedly took place here.

Photographers need a 300 mm lens to hunt portraits of deer and elk. Avoid disturbing them by close approach. A shorter telephoto can be used if the animals are to be an interesting foreground in a photo of distant high peaks early in the morning.

WINTER TRAIL 10
WINTER TRAVEL ON DEER MOUNTAIN

Type of trip: Out-and-back.
Total distance: 6 miles.
Maps: Trails Illustrated; Estes Park USGS quad.
Highlights: Views of Mummy Range and Front Range, picturesque limber pine, Deer Mountain summit (3 miles).
Wildlife: Mule deer, elk, black-billed magpie, mountain chickadee.
Deer Ridge Junction elevation: 8,930 feet.
Deer Mountain elevation: 10,013 feet.

Finding the trailhead: Begin hiking where US 34 and US 36 meet. There is no parking lot, but you can park along the broad shoulders.

The trip: At some time in almost every Rocky Mountain National Park winter, a long, warm, dry spell makes cross-country skiers and snowshoers despair and think of setting up banana farms near Estes Park. This is the time to hike up Deer Mountain, when you likely will encounter little snow.

During other times, such as when the skiing is good at Bear Lake or Glacier Basin Campground, the north-facing

Winter Travel on Deer Mountain

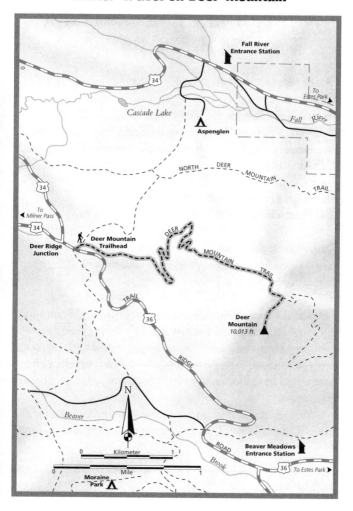

switchbacks on Deer Mountain will still have fairly deep snow. The zigzag nature of the trail causes climbers up Deer Mountain to move constantly from bare trail to snowy trail. On-off, on-off with skis or snowshoes is a significant nuisance.

Once on top, the trail usually holds snow in winter. But during the banana-belt periods, you may be able to walk a more or less dry route all the way. The trail undulates for more than a half mile along the mountaintop to a trail junction where a sharp right turn leads a few steep yards to the summit.

Many of the summer's best views from Deer Mountain are even better in winter. Snow on the high peaks of the Mummy Range to the north and Front Range to the south add considerable drama to these vistas. Low-angle winter light on the peaks gives the mountains more texture than in summer, although the shift of the sun to the south reduces the texture on the Mummy Range.

Ypsilon Mountain, with its classic bowl-shaped cirque cut by glaciers on its face, is the obvious center of interest among the high peaks closest to Deer Mountain. Of course, the Y-shaped pattern of snow-filled gullies that gave Ypsilon its name are far less obvious in winter when snow covers the whole face.

Where the trail levels atop Deer Mountain, forest fire has burned twisted limber pines, which are made even more interesting when snow accents the gray, rust, and black patterns. Low winter light is more likely than summer rays to emphasize the rough texture of the raised wood grain.

Mule deer are very common on Deer Mountain. Big bucks look their best in winter. By shredding bark from inoffensive young trees, the bucks have polished their antlers free of summer velvet. These dueling tools and coyote spikers shine in the winter sun.

WINTER TRAIL 11
TRAIL RIDGE ROAD

Type of trip: Out-and-back.
Total distance: 12 miles.
Maps: Trails Illustrated; Trail Ridge USGS quad.
Highlights: Views of the Mummy Range, wind-sculpted snow (4.2 miles), wind- and fire-sculpted trees (4.4 miles).
Wildlife: White-tailed ptarmigan, mountain chickadee, gray jay.
Many Parks Curve elevation: 9,620 feet.
Ute Crossing elevation: 11,440 feet.

Finding the trailhead: Follow Trail Ridge Road to its closure at Many Parks Curve.

The trip: Trail Ridge Road is closed above Many Parks Curve from late October through late May. Fairly easy to walk, the road is the easiest winter route to tree line in Rocky Mountain National Park. Tree line in winter is an interesting area and the place to find white-tailed ptarmigan in their all-white winter plumage.

Avalanche danger is slight; snowshoes or skis are probably unnecessary. Gaiters are handy for occasional wading through drifts, particularly between the open span of the old Hidden Valley ski slope and Rainbow Curve.

Wind can be a howling fury, particularly beyond Rainbow Curve, near tree line. Picking a day with good weather

Trail Ridge Road

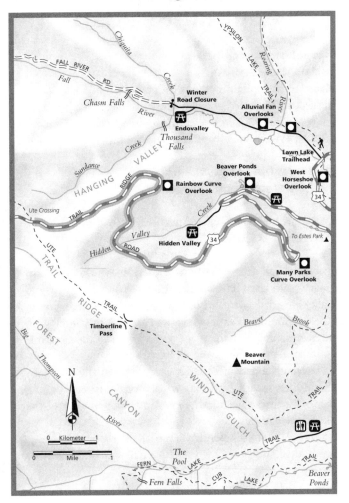

can make the difference between a trip remembered for exciting scenes and wildlife and one remembered for its misery.

The wind often carves snow drifts into interesting abstract patterns in the area of Rainbow Curve. During winter, the sun is low enough in the sky during most of the day to create dramatic shadows that accent the textures of these drifts.

Winter winds have given the trees above Rainbow Curve their fantastic shapes. Forest fire then accented and simplified the shapes by killing many trees. Snow further heightens the drama by covering up extraneous details.

Where the ridgeline narrows at tree line, large rock outcrops create a venturi effect. The same volume of air that has been moving across unobstructed tundra has to push through restricted space in the same amount of time. Therefore, the wind has to blow faster. Speeds well above 100 miles per hour are common and can knock you down. Wind chill can drop temperatures to decidedly dangerous levels, and frostbite is a common hazard. Linking arms with companions to fight your way across the venturi zone can be necessary on some days.

Look for ptarmigan by leaving the road above tree line at Ute Crossing, where a sign explains Native American travel across Trail Ridge. Head uphill across the road from the sign to look for the all-white grouse among scrub willows at tree line. Beware of going too near cliffs above Hanging Valley, particularly if windblown snow blocks your vision and unsteadies your balance.

WINTER TRAIL 12
WILD BASIN IN WINTER

Type of trip: Out-and-back.
Total distance: 7.4 miles.
Maps: Trails Illustrated; Allens Park USGS quad.
Highlights: North Saint Vrain Creek, Calypso Cascades (2.8 miles), Ouzel Falls (3.7 miles).
Wildlife: Mountain chickadee, red squirrel, snowshoe hare.
Winter Wild Basin Trailhead elevation: 8,350 feet.
Calypso Cascades elevation: 9,200 feet.
Ouzel Falls elevation: 9,450 feet.

Finding the trailhead: Eleven miles south of Estes Park, turn right (west) onto County Road 84W, the road to Wild Basin, which is marked by a sign along Colorado Highway 7. Drive 0.3 mile to an obvious right turn onto an unpaved road leading past the national park entrance station. The winter trailhead is a bit more than a mile down this road.

The trip: Even in midwinter, the quality of skiing or snowshoeing in the lower parts of Wild Basin depends on the heaviness of the most recent snowstorm. Relatively low altitude and south-facing exposure make snow on the trail patchy, particularly in spring. But north-facing slopes and heavily forested areas hold enough snow to make skis or snowshoes handy until late spring. Backcountry travelers probably will have to carry their skis or snowshoes over some bare sections.

Wild Basin in Winter

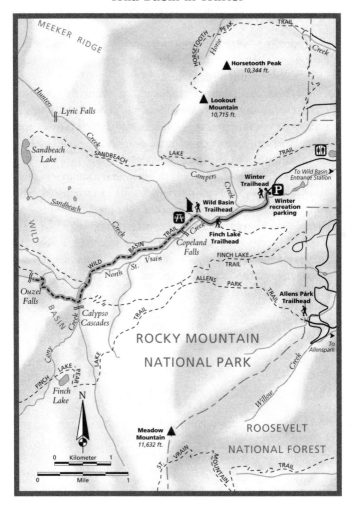

Avalanche danger is slight in Wild Basin for the first 6 or 7 miles, after which steep slopes create many slide paths.

From the winter parking area, which is about a mile east of the summer trailhead, follow the summer road along North Saint Vrain Creek.

Beyond the summer trailhead, the trail follows the creek even more closely than does the road. More than 2 miles from winter parking, a substantial bridge crosses the creek. Here the snow cover increases, and the trail steepens as it climbs to Calypso Cascades.

Cross Calypso Cascades (the bridge is usually evident above the snow) and pass through forest burned in 1978, where there are many opportunities for abstract photos of burned wood grain contrasting with the snow.

At Ouzel Creek leave the trail to trace the course of the creek a short way up to Ouzel Falls. Quieted from its summer roar, this waterfall freezes into patterns that rival its summer drama.